Widow, 44, Seeks Reader

Kate Rogers

Copyright © 2022 by Kate Rogers

All rights reserved. No part of this book may be reproduced or used in any manner without written permission of the copyright owner except for the use of quotations in a book review.

First Edition July 2022

Book design by Publishing Push

ISBNs
Paperback: 978-1-80227-562-9
eBook: 978-1-80227-615-2

Facebook: /kate.rogers.56808
Instagram: ba.rbie9411

Acknowledgements

With special thanks to Robert Timms for devoting time to helping this debut novelist to navigate the practical side to writing and getting published, specifically for editing the entire thing.

Thanks to the team at Publishing Push for guiding me to publication, being ever so patient with the whims of someone who acts like a kid in a candy shop when there are decisions to be made also to Brian Andrews for inspiring me to write this novel with the immortal words "you couldn't write this shit" – it turns out I could!

Thanks goes to Em Bamford for her continual constructive criticism, which may not always be constructive but is usually criticism and to all of my very special friends and family who helped me find my brighter days.

Dedicated to JuJu, one of the many I have loved and lost but who will always be the Judith to my Chalmers.

Chapter 1

'So, what could this adventure lead to?' thought Kate, as she sat waiting for the plastic surgeon to size her up and prep her for the surgery that lay ahead. Her breasts had always been ample, of course; 'more than a handful and more than an eyeful' was one particularly delightful, male-delivered, description she remembered from her earlier years. After the awkwardness of adolescence she grew to understand what a couple of assets she had, and despite the odd hiccup, such as having to reprimand the more blatant men for talking solely to her breasts, she found them to gain her a small sort of notoriety which she considered useful for gaining the edge in meeting people and being remembered.

Latterly, though, they had become more of a burden than an asset. To this end, Kate felt that the start of a new chapter was required. The irony wasn't lost on her: hospitals were a place she vowed she would avoid for ever, after losing Nick. But life had moved on and Kate felt sure that this was the key to reinventing herself. 'Because life is a series of reinventions, isn't it?' she thought, as the nurse was going through the very familiar standard health checks. Her thoughts were interrupted by the nurse.

'One hundred per cent oxygen level – you can't get better than that!' she exclaimed.

This jolted Kate back to those painful last weeks with Nick, watching him monitor his dwindling oxygen levels until, at the end, the carbon dioxide ably won the fight against the oxygen and Nick could simply no longer breathe. 'Anyway, back to reinventions,' Kate thought, in a bid to drag herself away from those dark memories.

There was the time she had reinvented herself as Madonna, shortly after the Lady Diana phase: off with the twin set and flicked hair, and on with the lace gloves and scraggy perm. Kate often wondered whether she and her friends were single-handedly responsible for the hole in the ozone layer, due to the sheer amount of hairspray they used in the 1980s. Or what about the time she had reinvented herself as a poet, writing endless thought-vomit during the university years?

So past reinventions may not have been the most successful – but what about the future?

Kate considered the bizarre situation she once again found herself in. It was fairly ill-thought-out by all accounts, as Kate found that when she devoted too much thought to something, she would almost certainly never do it. Waiting in the hospital that day, she pondered what bad luck it was to have such a good-looking doctor performing her surgery, not least when he arrived armed with several marker pens and proceeded to draw all over her upper body. Ten minutes later, while he was still creating a masterpiece of body art, Kate wondered whether things could get any more embarrassing. Of course they could, because Kate tried to break the embarrassment by making a humorous remark or two. What she received in response was: nothing. She concluded that this must be some sort of breast surgeon code of ethics; surely it couldn't simply be that she wasn't that funny! How weird it seemed to her that over the several appointments prior to today she had not realised quite how attractive the doctor was. Had fear blinded her on previous occasions? Perhaps he had recently partaken of plastic surgery himself, she thought, while giggling.

'Hi! I'm the anaesthetist,' announced another devastatingly handsome man who walked through the heavy wooden door an hour later. 'Well of course,' Kate thought, 'it couldn't possibly have been someone old, or ugly, or both. And just for good measure, both of these handsome individuals will later have the delight of seeing me in surgical stockings and not a lot else, oh joy!' For Kate, who had never been body-confident and was today required to show her boobs to every single person she met, this was a terrible situation. When changing at the gym she would go to great lengths to find a small cubby-hole, in order to avoid the embarrassment of showing any inch of flesh. She had once resorted to opening all the lockers down one side of the gym to form a makeshift door to undress behind – thereby drawing much more attention her way than if she had simply changed in public. She might as well have changed in the reception area! So while a breast reduction had felt like the right thing to do, as recurring health issues were not going to improve with age, this was all seriously testing Kate's metal.

At 44 years old, Kate found herself living comfortably in Kent. Things had been financially less comfortable six years ago, when she and husband Nick sold everything they owned and bought the house of their hopes and dreams, agreeing to a monstrous mortgage that would see them paying it off well into their seventies. They were hoping that 'something would come up' prior to that, so they could at least pay back the generous relatives who had helped fund the move – but they weren't sure *what* that would be, let alone *when*. So things had been precarious for a while.

Kate liked to be known as the creator of reinvention, but in practice she would only really reinvent herself if absolutely needed. She knew she was most comfortable in a pair of wellingtons, but equally she still adored the opportunity to dress up – Nick used to call her 'the magpie' due to her penchant for anything that glittered and sparkled. Ultimately Kate was a home-girl: happy to glam up, but even happier to strip off all the glitz and glam at the end of the night and return to PJs and wellingtons. After all, someone would have to give her horses their night-time snack. In fact, there was a ritual that Kate loved when stripping back the make-up after a night out. Hot chocolate in hand and a Marmite sandwich on the side, she would sing her favourite song:

> After the ball was ov–er,
> She took out her glass eye.

> Put her false teeth in wa–ter,
> Shook from her hair the dye.
> Kicked her cork leg in the cor–ner,
> Stripped off her false nails and all.
> Then what was left went to bye-byes,
> After the ball.

Surrounded by fabulous friends, a menagerie of pets and the rolling hills of the North Downs, what more could Kate ask for? Her life wasn't perfect – and she certainly didn't live in *Little House on the Prairie* – but it was well within the realms of sufficient. She had never stopped wondering what life could be like if she chucked it all in the air and did something radical; but to date, the nearest she had actually come to 'radical' was the surgery she was just about to have! However, her memories could last her a lifetime, and she and Nick had made it their mission to live life to the full at all times, 'just in case'.

This is the story of that 'just in case' moment when it came – and what happened afterwards.

Letter to Nick.

Is this misuse of the money you left me? This surgery isn't cheap, well out of range if you were still alive, but I just have to have it. So why do I feel so bloody guilty? Why has every waking hour for the last few weeks consumed me with dread that somehow you will come back from the grave and tell me off?! You never even told me off when you were alive, so why would you start now you're dead? Ok, I do realise that last-minute wobble when I started asking the surgeon about a facelift was a bit shallow, but I was panicking about coming through the general anaesthetic and thought I should get my money's worth. It was lucky the surgeon talked me down from that one in hindsight. So how do you feel about this reinvention of me so far?

Widow, 44
seeks someone.

Chapter 2

'I just want a sink in the downstairs loo for the wake,' sniffed Kate.

She was half-talking and half-sobbing to the tall plumber who had been recommended to her by her mother and sister. He was in fact highly rated and came by the nickname – unknown to him – of 'Fit Plumber'. Why? If Kate had to explain, she would say his height was part of the package, and he was an all-round nice guy – the dependable, level-headed, capable type… not to mention good-looking, too. Kate had phoned him, saying she had an urgent job that she would very much appreciate his help with. She had never met him before, yet he had met members of her family on several occasions, so the chances were that he was going to swing wide of her. But, to his credit, he did nothing of the sort, and arrived later that same day to assess the job.

When she called the plumber it had only been five days since Nick had died. Kate had had a moment of clarity: if the wake was going to take place in the building site of a house she lived in, there would be a requirement for a sink in the downstairs bathroom. Never mind the hideous Axminster carpet from the 1980s, or the immense amount of clutter that had inevitably built up while Nick was ill. Or the back door that would have leapt off its hinges if you gave it so much as a hard stare. People would just have to deal with those things – but a sink was absolutely necessary.

Kate realised that Fit Plumber was awaiting some sort of instruction.

'Oh, would you like a drink?' she asked, playing for time, as she wasn't sure what she had been halfway through saying when her mind had wandered. This was a trait she had distinctly noticed in the five long days since Nick's death: an absolute inability to concentrate on anything. No matter how big or small, retention of information completely evaded her at all times... She wondered if this was this the lack of—

'No, thanks,' interrupted his reply.

'Right. Oh,' continued Kate, 'the thing is, I can't show you the downstairs loo, as there's a spider in the way.' The words came out before she could stop them. 'You'll have to move it for me.' That was it now – Fit Plumber would unquestionably realise that Kate was related by blood to the rest of the family that he had met.

A few minutes later, spider moved and job looked at, Fit Plumber promised he would fit the job in prior to the wake. He started trying to back out through the front door while Kate was attempting to explain why the house was such a mess.

'Nice car,' he remarked on his way out, trying to lighten the situation – which turned out to be a big mistake. He was referring to Nick's precious kit car, the one he had been building until he got sick: a beautiful powder-blue car, which now sat forlornly on the driveway waiting for someone to love it and, more importantly, to finish building it.

'It was my late husband's,' Kate said, noticing she was using the term 'late husband' for the first time. 'He built it from scratch... Such long evenings... Meticulous attention to detail... So much pride... Zetec engine... Was going to race it.' It all came tumbling out in half-sobs, half-squeaks.

Realising that this was a pretty heavy situation for Fit Plumber to deal with on his first meeting with her, Kate tried to lighten the mood with humour: 'Well, I guess he won't race it now, will he?'

The effect of this, of course, was to make her more miserable and Fit Plumber more awkward. Could this get any worse?

The truth was that Kate didn't want to have to talk about U-bends with plumbers, or deal with spiders in her way. She didn't feel equipped to do so, or ready to communicate with the outside world at all. A huge black hole had opened up five days ago and she wanted to dive in head-first, never to be seen again. Didn't the universe realise that it was supposed to have stopped at exactly 4.03 a.m. that Sunday – at the moment Kate had uttered those fateful words, 'Oh, that's *brutal*'? In hindsight it seemed a strange choice of words to utter upon watching her precious husband die, but they came from the feeling of absolute injustice that something as automatic as breathing could suddenly evade someone like that – without much warning. Of course, Kate had known he was very ill; but she had thought there would be a more formal pronouncement of the impending end. So the term 'brutal' summed up exactly how she had felt: she and Nick had been brutally robbed of the life they loved. She hadn't rehearsed a fancy speech for such an occasion and therefore had to go with whatever came out in the moment. Being the master of random comments at inappropriate times and places, it could have been very much worse.

'Soooo… I'll see you in three days' time," ventured Fit Plumber, in a bid to round things off and get the hell out of the place.

'Yes, *please* come back,' begged Kate. As she turned around to shut the front door she caught a glimpse of herself in the window. 'Dishevelled' would be a generous way of describing her appearance, she thought. 'Utterly down and out' would probably be more accurate. Worn to a frazzle by several nights of not sleeping, Kate realised she had barely managed to dress herself, let alone wash or brush her hair. If other people could have done these things for her, they surely would have. No one envied her at that point, and absolutely everyone had offered 'whatever we can do'. 'It stretches beyond hair-washing and dressing, though,' she thought as she walked back into the house. 'But it could incorporate house work,' she said out loud with a wicked little grin, as she surveyed the mountain of washing-up and general debris around the newly-spacious kitchen.

Kate knew she should concentrate on at least *one* of the million things that needed doing, but could not decide which. Pages and pages of paperwork to wade through: forms to fill, documents to copy, envelopes to be addressed – just listing them made Kate want to run for the hills, screaming. She settled on finding pictures for the order of service. Photo albums piled up around her as she sat on the floor, desperately searching for those perfect pictures which summed Nick up in one stance, one glance, one smile. Kate was at least relieved that she had been so methodical in cataloguing photos over the years. Inevitably, as she worked her way through the many albums – an adulthood of glowing memories – her heart broke into several more fragments with each page. She finally settled on three pictures, which really showed the man Nick had been: fun, sporty and larger-than-life. 'You were so strong,' Kate told those images of Nick, while tears poured down her cheeks. She stared at the picture of Nick dressed in his Mr Strong T-shirt, with his bike held way above his head, on that bridge in Dartmouth. 'Fearless, too!' she mused, hugging the photo to her, unable to choke back the huge sobs that were welling up inside. Letting go, she threw herself back onto the floor and lay there weeping, allowing self-indulgence to completely take over for what seemed like forever. Eventually, however, the raw emotion subsided. All Kate was left with were sore eyes and a throbbing headache.

Letter to Nick.

To my darling Nick. There are so very many things that we left unsaid, which was right at the time for us both but leaves me feeling empty now. I would like to start by saying how very happy I am to have met you all those years ago. I grew in strength, self-confidence and as an all-round human being after meeting you, for which I am eternally grateful.

I must address my guilt at not spending enough time with you during your last few days and weeks. Please forgive me, as I bitterly regret that now. Sixteen years together and so many, many memories. Holidays, days out, promotions, job changes, gigs, parties, barbeques, walks, rides, surfs and just spending time together laughing and laughing and laughing.

You will always be my strength and my inspiration and I will always love you and miss you.

Widow, 42

seeks absolutely no one. Certainly not looking for love, companionship or even someone to breathe the same air with. *Had* good sense of humour, but does not feel she will see the funny side of anything ever again – therefore no sense of fun required. Please feel free to apply if you intend never to make contact, especially due to the fact that this lovely lady has yet to move into the twenty-first century, having no Facebook, Twitter or any other form of social media account whatsoever.

Chapter 3

The daily routine had quickly become familiar to Kate. It inescapably included opening the heart-warming numbers of sympathy cards that were arriving every day. Each one completely different both inside and out, Kate would read and re-read all of these, carefully soaking up the affection that each one emitted. Irrationally, the ones that began 'To Kate and Family' made her angry – they made her want to shout 'He was mine, no one else's!' The ones she liked the best contained anecdotes, things people remembered and loved about Nick.

Today's highlight was from one of Nick's work colleagues. It made Kate chuckle that it started 'Dear Mrs Rogers' – but better was yet to come, as this was a card of two halves, almost as though it referred to two completely different people in the picture it painted. 'I was so truly sorry to hear the news about Nick. The quiet dignity with which he endured his illness was amazing to witness.' Pride welled up in Kate and the emotion spilled over, making it difficult to read the next part. 'I shall remember him with fondness shouting "Jaegerbombs!" at the top of his voice at last year's Christmas party, just when the rest of us were ready for our beds.' What a tonic this was to Kate, to hear that the true spirit of Nick had not been lost amongst quiet dignity and enduring patience after all!

Arrangements for the funeral were going well. It had been particularly easy to choose everything for the day, as though it had all been prepared in advance, which it had not. No discussions had ever taken place over the previous year about end-of-life. It were as if a discussion of this nature would have hurried the end on, and therefore was taboo. Kate felt she was in suspended animation during the period leading up to the funeral. Her sole goal was to arrive, intact, at 17 June – past that, nothing registered or seemed to matter. The problem with nothing registering was that anything and everything had a strong chance of being forgotten. In a bid to counteract this, Kate had invested in several packs of bright pink sticky notes, to write important reminders on. Looking around her kitchen, she smiled at the overall effect they were starting to create on every work surface and cupboard door they had been stuck to, all shouting instructions at her: 'call plumber', 'take clothes to funeral director', 'put bins out'. From the mundane to the ridiculous, they unashamedly littered her beautiful new kitchen, but she didn't care in the least. 'All roads lead to 17 June – beyond that, who cares?' was the mantra which helped see her through those wretched first days.

'So, time for my walk,' announced Kate to no one apart from the cats, who had taken to moping round the house all day looking like lost souls. 'You're not helping!' she said to them, with fake annoyance, on her way out of the door. Walking was something that Kate had previously thought solely the domain of people who either didn't have a car or didn't have a life – weirdy-beardy hikers, for instance – but she had found walking to add a therapeutic effect to each day, especially during the glorious June weather. There had been no conscious decision to take up something therapeutic; just an urge to be doing something at all times, in order to avoid long hours of sitting and thinking. The sun was high in the sky and superbly warming on her face as Kate made her way along the beautiful green lanes towards the North Downs. Walking allowed time for healthy thinking, she found. Somehow the forward momentum of the physical activity allowed much the same for the thinking: ideas of what was to come, not what had passed. So, what *was* to come? Thoughts settled mainly on the funeral, of course, and the finer detail of what would happen on the day. Who would come? What would people say? How would she feel? What would she wear? Kate had a firm rule on attendance at funerals – black should be worn at all times – so that was a relatively easy decision. 'But how "together" should I look?' she asked herself while scrambling over the stile into the next field. 'I mean, if I turn up looking well-groomed, made-up and ready for anything, people might think I don't care about losing the love of my life,' she muttered. 'But if I turn up looking dishevelled, people will worry… Is there a middle ground?' Kate could not think what that middle ground might be – well turned out, but crawling into the crematorium on her knees in grief? Or perhaps she could don one of those black veiled hats to hide the hair and face? No, Victorian fashion was not for her, she concluded. 'I'll just have to make every effort – it's the least I can do,' decided Kate, as home came into sight once again.

Home had always been a welcome sight to Kate. 'Where the heart is' described how she felt about her beloved house; yet as she rounded the corner that day, there was no leap of the heart or feeling of pride that said: 'That's my house.' There was just nothingness, a mechanical feeling of 'this is where I dwell' – which saddened Kate even further, because nothing seemed to evoke any reaction in her at that time. There was a protective layer wrapped a thousand times around her – not the warm and fluffy kind, but the type that blotted out all sense of feeling, sight and sound. It was hard to comprehend how this would ever change. 'Is it a waiting game?' pondered Kate. 'Do I have to wake up a certain number of days until finally I wake up *feeling* something?' By nature Kate was an optimistic person, but she was struggling to see how this could possibly have a happy ending. As she arrived at the back door she found a beautiful potted delphinium of the brightest blue placed neatly on the ground. The accompanying card simply read: 'Thinking of you, xxx.'

Letter to Nick.

I have no more heart to clear out your bedside table than I would to kick a defenceless puppy. I looked today and staring back at me were your pants. Hilarious to think what an emotional attachment I seem to have to these mundane pieces of clothing but nevertheless I do, so they are certainly not for moving. I tried the next drawer and staring back at me were your black-rimmed glasses neatly residing in their blue case. This hurt even more, as glasses really defined you – I had never known you without glasses and by all accounts no one ever did, as you had worn them all your life. Seeing them there in the drawer with no purpose any more was a dagger to the heart. Funny how I feel like I am snooping through your stuff as I search further through this drawer, past the mountains of change, through the old watches and on to the cufflinks. I cannot even bear to go to the wardrobe or the drawers in there yet. They remain firmly shut and will do for some time.

Widow, 42

still seeks absolutely no one. *Had* a love of travel, but does not think this will ever happen again, due to lack of will and total uncertainty about what the future holds. She intends to see the brighter side of life at some stage in the future, but cannot currently comprehend anything beyond 17 June – so applicants, please, no contact prior to this date.

Chapter 4

Eventually 17 June – one of many pivotal days for Kate – arrived. She had focused her attention solely on that day for sixteen days since Nick's death, and now it was here. She was surprised to find that she awoke rather excited for the day ahead, and could not really fathom why. Who in their right mind would be excited about the day they got to say the last farewell to their life-long partner?

During the previous day Kate had been preoccupied with last-minute arrangements. There had been an excruciating situation in Sainsbury's, while shopping for the copious amounts of alcohol that would surely be needed to give Nick a fitting send-off. Walking about in a daze, picking up anything and everything that came to hand, she thought she had been doing quite well – until she arrived at the checkout. Bottle after bottle went through the scanner and into the bags, testing the capacity of her trolley.

'Having a party?' asked the chirpy young lad on the checkout.

'Burying my husband,' Kate replied, in a dead-pan monotone. She regretted it immediately. Her voice was so deep and devoid of emotion that she didn't even recognise it. It had not been a deliberate act of nastiness – but the effect had been the same. The poor young boy looked mortified, and Kate wanted the ground to swallow both of them up instantly. There was no coming back from that; there was absolutely nothing Kate could say or do to right the wrong, so she paid and left.

On many occasions afterwards she had sent that lad many virtual 'sorrys' in her head. It was perhaps a useful early lesson for Kate, showing that in fact the world did not revolve around her. Yes, a terrible thing had happened. Yes, it had ruined her happy world. But no, it was not acceptable to pass that on to everyone else along the way, and she should be mindful of that from now on.

Today the sun was shining over the beautiful green fields and Kate jumped out of bed for the day that she was so weirdly excited about. Soon people would start arriving: worried family, comforting friends, and everyone else who was feeling the loss just as much as Kate. A huge man-shaped gap had opened up in everyone's lives, and today they were all attempting to fill that gap – for one day only. No one knew what would happen *after* this day, but at least they could all cling to each other for a few hours and make some sort of sense of it all, temporarily.

As Kate carefully applied her make-up, dabbing the concealer blob by blob under her tired eyes, a voice came from behind her.

'You can't paint teardrops on.' It was Kate's sister. 'That's cheating!'

'Very funny,' was Kate's reply. 'I suppose *you'll* have to paint the teardrops on yourself, given that you never cry!'

It was true that Emily very rarely allowed her emotions to spill over. Nevertheless, she had been incredibly close to Nick, so Kate realised the possibility that her rebuttal had been a little harsh.

Everyone had started to arrive and the house was busy with the sound of chattering and tea-making. It was totally accepted in Kate's family that tea and/or sherry represented the cure-all in any situation, so both were flowing freely by ten o'clock.

'I think I'll have a gin and tonic,' announced Matt. Her brother was breaking with tradition – potentially leading Kate down a road that she knew would end in ruin if she wasn't careful.

'Me too,' she replied. Gin had been their grandad's favourite tipple, so it seemed wholly appropriate, as they stood in what had once been their grandparents' house, to honour that rival tradition. An inner voice spoke to her: 'Be careful today, Kate. You really do not want to be the entertainment at Nick's funeral.' But she brushed this away and considered that under extenuating circumstances one should be allowed to make different choices to normal days.

Although she reflected that the choice of gin and tonic was perhaps not that different to normal days.

Every room was taken. Guests were changing from their journey clothes to those of the respectful mourner, while catching up on recent goings-on and trying to act as normal as possible, avoiding the momentous event that was looming. There was a buzz of movement, a buzz of sound: the house was alive, and it felt good to Kate, except that she seemed to be hovering above it all as an observer. This wasn't a totally unpleasant feeling. It was just unusual for her not to be in the thick of things, feeling like a bystander or someone who was watching the scene on the television.

'What's the time?' she asked, for the hundredth time. This was her way of tuning back in to the situation.

Then it happened. The funeral car arrived, and Kate's excitement turned to utter fear, utter horror. Her legs gave way. She had always thought that when this happened in old movies it was just actors hamming it up. She had thought so up until that moment, when her legs actually failed her at the sight of Nick's coffin festooned with flowers. Luckily, her cousin Tom was there to steady her, which he did admirably, holding her tight until that initial moment had passed. The incident had probably lasted no more than ten seconds, but recalling it to this day, Kate could instantly cry and throw up all at once (a skill that had previously evaded her, and not one she was particularly proud to have learned).

Slowly, Kate walked out of the house to the waiting car, too scared to stare at the hearse bearing the coffin, for fear it would knock her legs from under her again. Ably assisted by Emily, they sat in the back of the car with a random old aunt of Nick's, though by then Kate's frame of mind was such that it could have been absolutely anyone. As they drove unhurriedly up the road Kate allowed herself to look at the car ahead. She saw the flowers she had commissioned, simply saying 'NICK', laid at the back of the coffin; those four letters crushed her heart so tightly she thought she would stop breathing altogether.

As she clung to Emily, dabbing the tears away as best she could, a conversation in front of her broke through her thoughts and she wondered if she could possibly be hearing what she thought she was hearing. Nick's father and brother were in the row in front of them and she distinctly heard their speculation: 'Well, she's young. She'll marry again.' Kate was incredulous. What sort of conversation was this on the way to Nick's funeral? Luckily, raw emotion choked back what she wanted to say at that point, so the moment passed without incident. But she was left thinking that these two intrinsically kind-hearted people should never be allowed out in public!

The journey to the crematorium was intensely hot, as it appeared that 17 June had decided to be the hottest day of the year. In many ways this was just what Kate had hoped for, in order that the wake could largely take place in her beautiful garden at home. However, it made for an airless journey in a stiflingly hot car, worsened by her insistence on the traditional black garb, head-to-foot. As they pulled slowly through the wrought-iron gates of the crematorium, Kate lowered the window further and stuck her head out for air. She caught sight of the huge crowd of people waiting outside the chapel at the far end of the drive, and was suddenly overwhelmed with fear.

'Stop!' she shouted, causing the car to screech to a halt (which was somehow possible, even at only twenty miles per hour). 'I need a wee.'

Letter to Nick.

We all came to celebrate your life today. So many people that there was standing room only in the chapel – well done you on drawing a decent crowd! The whole occasion was thoroughly enjoyable, being back in a moment when you actually felt so close again. I'm not sure what the huge crowd of mourners thought when the funeral car screeched to halt and I got out and bolted down the drive for a wee – it must have been that bloody gin!

Widow, 42
seeks 'new husband', as decreed by father-in-law and brother-in-law during trip to funeral. Applicants need not apply at this stage, as period of mourning is yet to be determined, but thought likely to be in excess of 100 years.

Chapter 5

'Have you met my oldest living friend?' asked Kate slightly tipsily, introducing her boss to Katherine.

It was nothing less than an ambush, really. The subject of returning to work had innocently cropped up in conversation after the funeral and Kate had panicked. In looking for a rock-solid ally she had settled on Katherine – they had been friends since first meeting at university twenty years ago. Katherine had been the first one on the doorstep the day after Nick had died, and had been there in spirit throughout. Every day a little card, a text or a phone call would remind Kate that Katherine was there for her, willing and able to tread every step of this thing called grief with her. Somewhere along their twenty-year timeline, Katherine had got used to being introduced to new people by Kate as her 'oldest living friend'. Even though it was on many counts inaccurate, it was fun and had actually been adopted by Katherine as a standard way of introducing herself.

'Pleased to meet you,' replied Neil – rather too formally, as was his usual way.

'Tell him, Katherine!' begged Kate. 'Tell him I can't possibly go back to work yet. We have things planned for at least the next couple of weeks.'

Neil sensed not only Kate's panic but also the fact that entering into a debate with these two strong, independent women might be more than a match for him. He immediately backed down on the subject, muttering something about 'far too soon, no pressure'. As they watched him scuttle off, Kate and Katherine giggled conspiratorially and hugged.

The house and garden were full to bursting; absolutely everyone had come back from the crematorium to toast Nick's life. It was a comforting blanket around Kate all day. Even after the sun had set and the night air drew in, she felt totally enveloped by the warmth of people's wishes and love.

'Should widows smile so much on their husband's funeral day?' she asked her sister.

'Depends what they've inherited!' was the mercenary reply from Emily.

Later that evening the last few remaining mourners gathered in a circle on the lawn, drinking sherry and eating Chinese takeaway. Sitting on the motley array of garden chairs they reminisced, they joked and they laughed. They were clinging to each other in order to make sense of it all. Kate treasured that day for weeks and months to come, because in the morning the hugest black hole opened up in her life, which she could not escape for all the world.

In stark contrast to the previous day, Kate awoke feeling lifeless on 18 June. It was as though her legs were made of lead. Even thinking about swinging them out of bed was out of the question. When she did finally make it up she realised that this was no ordinary hangover; it was quite simply a black hole that she was falling into, with absolutely no way out. 'Where's the bloody ladder?' she thought, as she felt herself slip further and further in. But there was no stopping it. One by one her guests left the house that day, and with each one Kate slipped a little further – until, after looking out of the back window at the garden full of the previous day's floral tributes, Kate finally gave in and went back to bed.

Several dark, uneventful days passed until Kate realised that she really needed to find that ladder. She decided to contact a counsellor, to help her climb out of the black hole. Kate also considered that work would be much happier if they felt she was actually taking steps to rehabilitate herself back to a better frame of mind – a frame of mind which might see her return to work at some stage before the end of the century. Her employers had been more than understanding and were exerting no pressure whatsoever. But Kate felt this was the least she could offer in return, so her decision was made. 'It can do no harm, and might just help,' she reasoned while dialling the number.

It turned out that this was a telephone triage service and therefore she faced a series of questions. 'Excellent!' thought Kate. 'This is my best subject, as I will know all the answers about myself!' But nothing had prepared her for the question that followed.

'Have you harmed, or are you considering harming, yourself?' asked the triage operator on the call.

A long pause ensued as Kate processed this question. 'Oh my God!' came her reply. 'I need a little help, but I'm not barking mad.' Kate was never one to make understatements; this accurately conveyed how she felt about the question. It had jolted her somewhat into thinking about the poor people out there who were really desperate – rather than just desperately unhappy, as she was.

After a little more questioning the triage operator concluded with a plan. 'So, we'll book you in for a series of four face-to-face sessions with our counsellor Audrey. The first one will be on Friday at two o'clock.'

When Friday came, Kate decided to visit her friend Alison on the way, as 'tea and sympathy' had been offered previously. Tea was duly served and there was much chattering about life in general and what a lovely summer it was turning out to be. This was very true: since Nick's passing the sun had shone solidly for the whole month of June, unabated by even the slightest hint of a cloud.

'I'm off to see a counsellor this afternoon,' Kate announced, fully expecting some sort of affirmation of her actions from Alison.

'Really?' came the shocked reply. 'I thought you were such a "together" person. Why would you do that?'

Kate was in disbelief. This was the first time that someone had questioned her actions since Nick had died. In principle Kate welcomed a return to reality – but sadly this was neither the time nor the subject for such a return. Smarting and feeling she had to justify herself, Kate simply replied: 'That's exactly *why* I'm doing it. I want to *stay* "together".'

With this she made her excuses. As Kate left she considered that the offer of tea and sympathy had been a false one – it was merely tea with a little judgement on the side. Alison had tried to go on and defend her position, explaining that she had never gone for counselling when her father had passed away all those years ago. Kate had wanted to retort, 'Perhaps that's why you suffer so badly with OCD' – but refrained, and was later thankful for that rare moment of self-control and actually a little sad for Alison that she couldn't see that for herself.

Kate arrived at the medical centre where the counsellor was based. It was a small, rather grubby place in a dirty old local town, one of the many in area that was down on its luck. She would have preferred a calming new-age purpose-built facility – not one that required you to literally fight for a space to park and then made you feel like you might catch something really nasty if you spent too much time in the building. The receptionist pointed her upstairs – a direction confirmed by the signage – and she slowly dragged herself up the open-slatted staircase. The ascent was painfully slow, as she once again had those lead weights strapped to her legs. Perhaps it was fear of the unknown or a recognition that she might have to face things she didn't want to that afternoon.

As she sat and waited for the counsellor to call her in, Kate looked around. An NHS dentist; a speech therapy unit, with a happy little family talking animatedly about their daughter's progress since the last visit; an STD clinic. What an eclectic mix.

'Kate?' said a small voice.

Kate thought it seemed to be coming from entirely the wrong person. Approaching her was a tiny-framed lady of about fifty, dressed in a sharp, fitted suit dating from about 1990. She had long brown hair which was loose yet concertedly doing what it was told – a feat Kate could never manage with her own, slightly wild blonde hair. This was not at all what Kate had imagined when they had told her she would be seeing 'Audrey the counsellor'. She had imagined a large lady with wild grey hair dressed in a black kaftan, floating ethereally everywhere in bare feet. Instead, Audrey's leopard-print kitten heels clack-clacked in front of Kate as they walked towards the room where they would be spending the next hour.

The room was no less of a disappointment. Once again Kate had imagined something very different: a large airy space with light streaming through the windows and large floor cushions scattered everywhere. Instead, she stepped into a small dark room that smelt a little musty and evoked all the comfort and serenity of a broom cupboard.

Despite terrible first impressions, which Kate had quickly resolved to put behind her, as it was simply a matter of her imagination versus reality, that first counselling session worked well. It set the scene in allowing her to speak freely, in a way that she simply could not with anyone else. There were still things that she wouldn't allow herself to think, let alone say, but she was sure this would come – and if it didn't then perhaps it didn't need to. It turned out that afternoon that one of her primary concerns was that she felt she would never feel enjoyment to 100% again. She could still laugh and see the funny side of things, but even the funniest moment, joke or comment would only evoke 50% enjoyment now, compared to before. She was worried that this would be life for ever more. So as Kate left that first hour, she felt satisfied that more counselling sessions would be useful. She was even looking forward to going again in two weeks' time.

Letter to Nick.

I have been stuck at the bottom of a black hole for weeks now and can see absolutely no way out. I can't even see a ladder, let alone reach it. The hole has sheer sides and it's slippery like an eel and so dark that I have to leave lights on all over the house at all times now. Night-time TV is dragging me into its web – the hours of 2 a.m. till 4 a.m. are the best/worst.

I had a dream about you last night. We were at a party and I said something crap like 'Oh, I thought you were dead.' But you couldn't hear me, no matter how loudly I shouted.

Widow, 42
seeks solace. Likely only to be found in oldest living friends. Eligible bachelors need not apply, as she would neither see you nor want to engage with you in any way.

Chapter 6

Counselling had helped Kate decide what she *didn't* want, and that was to return to work too soon. She had decided that she needed to do the counselling thing while cocooned in her bubble of surreal existence – a bubble which required her to stay away from everyday life. She was a functioning human being, but not ready to take back the demands of full-time employment, so she resolved she would have to speak to her boss.

A date was agreed to meet the following week, in Harlow of all places – 'Talk about kicking a person when they're down!' she thought, with a small return to her old sense of humour. The meeting was entirely uncomfortable, as it turned out that Kate could utter no more than five words in a row before breaking into tears. Neil handled the situation admirably, for a person who by nature was socially awkward at the best of times, and the conclusion was that Kate would come back to work in September.

The weight that lifted from Kate as she drove away from that meeting was immense, as she really felt she could devote time to the job of healing without distraction or worry, which was a major breakthrough. She even giggled a little when she thought about Neil's slightly panicked face when she had burst into tears – before she had nearly fallen backwards off her chair in her hurry to rush to the ladies' cloakroom to compose herself. She continued to giggle as she realised that the timeframe she had put on returning to work basically meant she would be taking the whole summer off. Result! Eight long weeks lay ahead of her at this point. The possibilities were endless; but where should she start?

Pilates seemed like the obvious first choice, as Kate had felt for some time that the physical benefits of this pursuit would really help her, but somehow she had never made time to try it. One of the reasons she hadn't gone before was that it seemed to be mainly the domain of people who had spare time during the day. But now she could legitimately join that community, so she found a local group and signed up.

Arriving at the tiny village hall for the first session, Kate was not at all surprised to find that the group consisted exclusively of ladies of mature years. 'This should be Ok,' she thought. 'I must be at least thirty years younger than any of them, so I shouldn't get left too far behind.' After all, Kate was a fairly active person: she rode her horse regularly, swam whenever the opportunity arose, and had been walking regularly now for a good five weeks. The first routine was obviously well known to all of the group except Kate. 'That's fine, I can muddle through,' she said to herself, while performing another Swan Dive. 'This is actually quite easy.'

Ten minutes later – as she laid on her back, physically unable to lift her own body weight up, with her arms seemingly useless – she looked around her. Every single old lady, even the one who walked with a Zimmer frame, could do this move. Frustration built up and as she huffed and puffed, resorting to a little cheating use of her hands, she finally made it to a sitting position. She had performed only one of these dreaded roll-ups to the ten that the rest of the group had achieved.

'What's wrong with me?' she complained aloud.

'You just need to build your core strength,' the instructor replied. This Kate understood, but really, she could do no more than lift her head off the mat. Did she have marshmallow where her core should be?

Staggering out of the class an hour after she had skipped in, Kate realised she had grossly miscalculated how unfit she had become during those long months when Nick had been ill. Pilates was just the start; she needed to get serious about doing more. Time was available to her now and she had to use it before work got seriously back in the way again.

With limited time in mind she also indulged in her first foray into aesthetic improvements. Wonky teeth had never fazed her as a youngster. In fact, she had tried braces in her early teens but ditched them within a few days, on the basis that life was for living – not for watching what you ate or worrying about how you looked in a photo. This attitude had largely stayed with Kate throughout her adult life, until she registered with her current dentist five years ago, when an inevitable sales push had made her start to reconsider her stance. Over the subsequent years she had grown to loathe her crooked teeth. Now she decided that with disposable income in her pocket, the most important thing she could attend to would be to get braces!

'What a weird reaction to losing your husband,' she thought as she left the orthodontist, complete with the latest in discreet adult braces. 'Still, at least you'll stick these ones out, because you're in it for two thousand pounds this time!'

Looking back, Kate often thought that her friends and family must have been worried at this time. Within a month of losing Nick she had virtually quit her job (albeit until September), taken up pilates, found a new love of the previously-hated walking, started counselling and had braces fitted to her teeth. If they did worry then they didn't show it. Perhaps there were secret summits behind closed doors; perhaps they just trusted that Kate would navigate this path her own way.

The summer stretched out ahead of her, and Kate was looking for yet another distraction. As they lazed in the sun one July afternoon her sister-in-law suggested turning Kate's new-found love of walking into a charity fundraiser.

'There's a night-time walk in London in September,' suggested Clare, 'called Shine London. I think it's thirteen miles – why don't we do that?'

Thus the latest plan was born, and along with the support of her good friend and neighbour Lou, they started training. Or at least 'training' was what they called it. It was rare if they managed more than eight miles during their 'training' walks. Sometimes pubs would be the distraction, and sometimes tea and cake; whatever it was, there was *always* a distraction. Meanwhile they set up their fundraising pages, and Kate felt sure that with sympathy running high her totals would be good, so she set a stretch target of £250 on JustGiving. Underneath a photo of her feet – in which she had painted her toenails an array of colours – a heartbroken message announced the event:

> See those feet? They're not great but they are going to walk 13 miles to help beat lung cancer in Nick's memory. We have to fight the vile disease that took him and with your help we might just help the 43,500 people that are diagnosed with lung cancer each year. I am pretty sure Nick would laugh to see me of all people walking a half-marathon with my dodgy old feet but I would walk a marathon every day if I thought it would help make breakthroughs in combatting this terrible disease. Please dig deep.

The donations were endless and generous and all accompanied by messages of support and love. They formed another blanket for Kate, bringing back the warmth of hope that she had last felt on the day of the funeral. Her favourite message from one of the donors read: '…and I would walk 500 miles and I would walk 500 more…' This summed up exactly how Kate had felt when writing her JustGiving description for would-be donors. She thought the most random message was that from her cousin Lottie: 'Next challenge: rebuild Hadrian's Wall!' And then there was the inevitable one from Emily, which simply read: 'Go fast so we can have a pint at the finish.'

Letter to Nick.

Thanks for being considerate enough to die in the summer so at least bereavement leave could be spent outside. I have made such a good fist of grieving in the sun that Rachel declared I looked like a 'blonde-haired Jamaican' when she came to stay last weekend! I know it won't look good to return to work looking tanned, refreshed and with newly fitted braces on my teeth - people will think I've been on a health spa retreat. Perhaps I'd better rough myself up a bit before I go back.

I tried to look in the wardrobe again today but the sight of your suits was enough to make me close it up tight and make a cup of tea - another time, maybe.

Widow, 42
seeks blister plasters!

Chapter 7

With only twenty-nine days until her return to work, Kate decided that a little holiday would be the best thing to book next. There had been plenty of days out up till then: her mother was always happy to oblige with trips to garden centres (especially if there was a coffee shop attached) and with general retail therapy, and there had even been visits to a bird of prey sanctuary and a mini-safari at the nearby wildlife park. In fact, the wildlife park had been an exceptional outing in the end. They had loved such a diversity of animals and it had been so wonderful to have the time to just wander aimlessly all day, with no time constraints or places to have to get to. The gorilla enclosure was so impressive that they had decided to double-back at the end of the day for another opportunity to stare at these amazing creatures. Their luck had been in, as the keepers were just feeding them. Kate and her mother had marvelled at how dextrous the gorillas were, gathering up all the fruit and vegetables in order to make their own personalised afternoon snacks. The big silverback, nearest to them, had been so magnificent that Kate had decided to take a selfie with him. Pulling a suitable 'scared' face, she had fiddled around for ages, trying to hold the phone and press the button simultaneously, during which time Mr Silverback had taken exception to her invading his space. Unknown to Kate, concentrating hard on not dropping her phone, he had picked up a stick that was close to the bars of the enclosure. He had then hurled it directly at her, making her jump so much that she had flung her phone up in the air, before running for her life. When she had stopped and looked back, after putting a clear fifty feet between her and the enclosure, what Kate saw had dismayed her: there must have been at least twenty people crying with laughter at the whole scene. 'Once again,' she had thought, 'the joke is not only *on* me but *is* me!' So the days out had been fun – for some people – but Kate felt like something longer was needed.

The destination she settled on was Cornwall, a place that held many happy memories for her, as she and Nick had taken some crazy and wonderful trips there over the years. It was all planned for the bank holiday weekend in August: a three-night stay was deemed just enough time to relax and have some fun, but not so much time that Kate, Emily and their mother might start seriously annoying each other. This was a well-laid plan, but in reality just one night tested everyone's patience, before they had even arrived in the county of Cornwall.

Staying at a small hotel en route to their final destination was deemed the sensible thing to do, as Emily had needed to work that day, so they couldn't leave until the afternoon. A slow journey through Friday afternoon traffic had done nothing for their mood, and the sight of their accommodation did not particularly lift their spirits. It was one of those functional hotels sited at a Services area just off the dual carriageway, which had ticked the 'cheap' and 'well-located' boxes but not necessarily the 'cheerful' box.

'Never mind,' Kate told the others. 'It's just a resting place for a few hours, so we can get a nice early start tomorrow morning.'

Then of course there was the question of sleeping arrangements. Thrifty Kate had only booked one family room – they *were* family, after all – but that meant one double bed and one single bed. So who would be sharing? Kate and Emily must have had this thought at exactly the same moment, as they swung open the door to the room and both bolted for the single bed. Caught in the rush, their mother was not only pushed aside but right through the bathroom door. Kate made it to the bed first, but in her determination she had flung herself at it so vigorously that she bounced right off, crashing to the floor with a thud. So Emily claimed victory – but in the end they both had to relinquish the prize of the single bed to their mother, who ruled that her bruised elbow had been a result of her daughters' 'bad behaviour'. Despite a bad start, the rest of the evening passed off uneventfully, so all three of them were looking forward to their luxury long weekend.

Kate realised that the Cornwall trip represented another milestone: an opportunity to discover the healing power of… spa breaks! Technically, they were not actually discovering this power for the first time, but 're-discovery can be just as powerful as discovery,' Kate concluded. The spa hotel overlooked the famous Fistral beach near Newquay – not that any of them could tell this upon arrival, due to the typical August bank holiday weather of squally showers punctuated by torrential rain. The weather was not a deal-breaker for the three of them, however, as they unpacked and headed to the bar for the first drink of their holiday.

'Oooh, cocktails!' cried Kate excitedly. 'Let's have one while we choose our spa treatments.'

'Mine's a penis colada,' replied Emily without hesitation, cracking the same joke that they had used for as long as Kate could remember.

As they settled down in the lounge to peruse the spa treatment brochure, Kate's phone rang. It was her boss.

'Bloody cheek,' said Emily when she saw Neil's name flash up.

'Hardly,' said Kate. 'I've been off work since the first of June, for God's sake, and they haven't quibbled about a single thing so far – they couldn't have been nicer.'

Emily huffed, which was her standard response to anything related to work. This was a transference of her own workplace frustrations, assuming that everyone else must be just as unhappy in their jobs as she was. On Sunday evenings Emily would regularly descend into a fit of depression at the thought of going to work the next morning, and would start frantically checking her lottery numbers and asking everyone else whether they had also bought lottery tickets that weekend – and if not, why not.

'I'll call him back after our trip,' said Kate, knowing that her very understanding boss would be totally fine with that.

Cocktails enjoyed and spa treatments booked, Kate sat on her bed while Emily hogged the bathroom. They had agreed to share and let their mother have the single room after the incident the night before, as Mum had not let them forget her 'hideous' elbow bruise all day. Kate chuckled while remembering the last time they had been to a spa hotel, which had been during a ski trip the previous year. As a special treat they had decided to book a massage for the final day of the holiday and had excitedly arrived at the treatment rooms to be told that they would be sharing a room, which was not their idea of relaxing. However, they had decided to make the best of the situation and, sticking to the strict 'no looking' rules which Emily had established and Kate had been more than happy with, they had quickly changed into paper pants and had laid down on their respective couches. Both of them had started the treatment with a fit of the giggles, when two enormous burly women had arrived and asked them in broken English 'how hard they liked it'. Kate had then relaxed and started to enjoy the aches and pains of the week's skiing being over-zealously pummelled out of her. Meanwhile Emily had started letting out little squeaks, every time her therapist caught one of the many bruises she had picked up that week when learning to snowboard. Suddenly Kate's therapist had walked to the end of the couch to stand facing Kate's feet, before vaulting onto the couch on top of Kate, quite literally mounting her! This had simply been too much for Emily, who had burst into fits of laughter, which in turn had started Kate laughing too.

'What are you laughing at, you weirdo?'

Emily's question interrupted Kate's memory, bringing her back to Cornwall. This question, although simple, hit Kate with significance: 'I'm *laughing*,' she thought. 'What a breakthrough!'

That evening they decided to eat at the hotel restaurant but, naturally, stopped at the bar first for pre-dinner drinks. The panoramic windows provided superb views over the golden sands below, and the evening was so beautifully sunlit that Kate felt the beach could have been anywhere in the world. Much to their delight the bar offered an impressive array of cocktails. They made their choices very quickly, then settled at a window table to take in the breathtaking scenery. It was agreed that the following day they would hire bikes in Padstow and ride the Camel Trail, before treating themselves to dinner at Jamie Oliver's restaurant in Watergate Bay.

Dinner that night was a blur to Kate; the cocktails before and afterwards were free-flowing, as was the wine during the meal itself. She concluded that she had enjoyed herself thoroughly, and found that alcohol plus fresh Cornish air, combined with having Emily sharing the room, made for the first good night's sleep Kate had managed in weeks. Good for Kate, it seemed, but not so for Emily, who complained bitterly the next morning about Kate's snoring.

Padstow was a bustling village of delights on Sunday, offering Kate, Emily and their mother just the break from normal life that they all needed after the trauma of the past few weeks. There was one small hiccup when, of all possible coincidences, Kate spotted a colleague from work – but Kate turned on her heels and avoided having to communicate with him. The subsequent fear she had felt at nearly having bumped into him made Kate realise just how difficult a return to work was going to be. However, that thought was quickly shoved to the back of her mind by a large Cornish pasty and a bottle of near-lethal Rattler cider. It turned out that drinking cider before riding a bike was not conducive to an altogether successful trail ride. Kate managed to fall off her bike no fewer than three times before they actually left Padstow, although she would not have it that cider was the cause.

'I just haven't been on a bike for ages,' she protested when Emily accused her of being a drunken bum.

'Well, it's a lot like riding a bike...' retorted Emily, speeding off.

Cornwall threw the usual extremes of weather at them during their short stay: they were scorched by sun while riding bikes in Padstow; drenched by the rain during a walk along the beach; and then well and truly exfoliated by the sand on the way down to the sea for some fairly unimpressive surfing. But all of that was inconsequential once they hit the spa again on Monday afternoon. 'Yes, tranquillity is what I need,' thought Kate. 'That and a nice massage.'

Letter to Nick.

I felt you there in Cornwall, Nick. But it's still too raw to allow myself to really consider what life will be like for more than one day at a time. I guess the thought that you are watching over me is much more comforting than you simply not being around now or ever again.

I find myself listening to Fleetwood Mac all the time, playing 'The Chain' on a loop for hours on end, singing every word, feeling every single beat of the music and remembering how it seemed to bring me so close to you as it played at the funeral. In filed friends and family... 10, 20, 30, 50, 100... I lost count while Lindsey Buckingham and co sung their hearts out. It brings back memories of that last happy gig we went to, the power of the music which made us forget for a few delightful hours how you were wasting away, losing the fight despite giving it everything you had.

I miss you Nick, so much.

Widow, 42
seeks loads more experiences that she can justify under the banner of 'Nick would have wanted me to'. No companions required other than those already known to her. Strangers beware.

Chapter 8

The Cornwall break did much to restore Kate's confidence in the fact that she might have the ability to enjoy things to more than 50% now and then, which was a welcome step forward after twelve weeks of wondering. They had packed the days and evenings of their long weekend with everything they enjoyed, frequently invoking the phrase 'Nick would have wanted us to' – a way of justifying any amount of money spent on absolutely anything, which, it turned out, was a slippery slope.

Kate realised that she owed her boss a phone call upon returning home, having unceremoniously ignored him while they were in Cornwall. She had been left with no choice after Emily had threatened to throw her phone in the sea if she answered any work calls at all. Kate appreciated the tough-love sentiment that her sister had been trying to convey, in helping her to disconnect for a while in order to truly heal. She was, however, in no doubt that Emily would have actually carried out the threat, recalling the time one Christmas when Emily had grabbed Kate's phone and declared it was 'time for a little game'. She had swiftly typed a text message saying 'Get yr hair cut u bummer' and sent it to a random entry in Kate's address book. As it was her work phone, Kate had been relieved to find that the recipient was at least somebody less senior than her. Nevertheless it had still been an awkward conversation on the Monday morning to explain what had happened. Kate had found herself using phrases such as 'Of course, you have lovely hair, it doesn't need cutting at all,' while trying to justify how irresponsible she had been in allowing her dysfunctional sister to get hold of her mobile. Kate had often thought that her whole career had been founded on shaky ground in this sense anyway – people seemed to think she was far more sensible and responsible than she was – which disconcerted her regularly. The Christmas incident had been yet another reminder of this, so in Cornwall she had taken Emily at her word and refrained from calling her boss back until after the bank holiday weekend.

As Kate tapped the 'call' icon she was slightly nervous. She wondered why. She had worked with Neil for years, but somehow this momentous event in her life had changed everything. Everyday situations and relationships had become unfamiliar to her overnight. It was like learning to walk and talk again; not that she remembered the first time round, of course. There was also the awkwardness of the very beginning of each conversation, when an innocent 'How are you?' could provoke a million different responses, depending on how the day was going. Kate recalled the many times people had floored her with that one simple question over the previous weeks – acres of silence would lie in front of her as she tried to muster some sort of response, sometimes so choked it felt like someone had their hands squeezed tightly round her throat. Then there were those times when her attempts to contain the emotion exploded into some sort of snot-snort down the phone; looking back, Kate felt that must have been pretty terrifying for the person on the other end of the line.

'Hello?' Neil answered tentatively. 'How are you, Kate?'

'Oh no, the dreaded question,' thought Kate. Luckily, though, she was feeling revived after the break in Cornwall so no snot-snorts were forthcoming. They chatted fairly casually for a few minutes about what each had been doing since they had last talked several weeks earlier. There had been lots of changes at work since Kate had been off and she wondered if she would have the strength to cope with all the changes on top of all the inevitable 'firsts'. First meeting with friends and colleagues. First national meeting (coming up soon) where she would feel so exposed, with everyone secretly looking at her and wondering what it was like to have your life torn apart unexpectedly. First business trip away with no one to come home to.

Kate's thoughts were suddenly interrupted: 'So shall I go ahead with the interviews then?'

'Sorry, Neil,' Kate replied truthfully. 'I zoned out for a moment. Interviews?'

No fewer than three people had left Kate's team while she had been off work.

'Three people in three months?' she asked. 'What the hell have you done to them?' As Kate quizzed Neil she felt some of her old spark returning. Of course, it was nothing Neil had done; it was simply circumstantial that those three people had been ready for moves within the business just when opportunities had arisen.

'Just my bloody luck,' she concluded.

'So, as I say, I am more than happy to screen CVs and do the interviews for you,' Kate heard Neil saying, as she wondered what her team would be like with half of them missing.

'God, no!' replied Kate before she could stop herself, thinking that there was no way she would want any 'Neil clones' anywhere near her team. Neil was a good man but was also Kate's polar opposite, living – it seemed to her – in a world of spreadsheets, analytics and procrastination. If she came back to work with half her team filled with his type of person, it might just tip her over the edge. 'I'd much rather conduct the process myself,' Kate went on, a little more diplomatically.

Right there was the jolt Kate had needed: the point at which she decided that she must step outside the protective cocoon of the past three months. In eight days' time she would be returning to work, and this was the first moment when she had allowed herself to properly consider the fact.

What to do with those eight precious days? How had three months passed by so quickly – and yet, at times, so painfully slowly? It was simple. The glorious summer days had been filled with anything and everything Kate loved to do. It had been her way of feeding the 'feel good' factor, to try and outweigh the 'feel bad' factor whenever it came. It had been as though she had to force the balance of the scales heavily in favour of 'Ok' so that she could control the scales when they tipped back towards 'Not Ok'. To this end the days had usually been packed with walking in the sun, eating ice cream, swimming, gardening, long lunches with friends; her list went on. The 'Not Ok' came mainly at night, when the door was closed on those long luxurious days and Kate was left in the house on her own. No matter what time that was, the heaviness would descend, with doubt, fear and loneliness creeping into Kate's world. Generally unaccustomed to any of these feelings previously, she found them pervading her nights like unwelcome visitors; try as she might, they wouldn't leave until daybreak. In her attempts to evict them she had taken to watching an array of never-ending Sky TV channels. As a result she had become an expert on the pawnbroking industry in the US, on the movements of various police forces across the UK, and on the curious, yet strangely entertaining, lives of children who competed in beauty pageants. Emily had mercilessly taunted her over her viewing habits during that time – but these channels had been her friend and had seen off the unwelcome early hours of every morning.

Kate had also relied heavily on the Macmillan Cancer Support chatroom during those months, avidly reading stories of similarly bereft people and realising that, in relative terms, she could be much worse off. Like the lady who had lost not only her husband but also her house, due to the financial situation she found herself in. Or the blogger who had no surviving family and whose friends had then seemed to drift away. 'How is that even bearable?' Kate sobbed. This was so often her reaction to the nightly ritual of reading the blogs and messages of all the poor souls out there. There was one blogger in particular who grabbed Kate's attention, a lady who had lost her soul-mate only three weeks after Kate had lost Nick. Kate had struck up a friendship with her through the online community and they would contact each other regularly with messages of support and stories from the latest experiences of their newly-acquired widowhood. She later found a message she had written to her new friend at that time, which summed up perfectly the state of their friendship in those early days, after the horror of each friend losing the love of her life:

> *Dear Queen Dawn! I love the idea of you being shocked at the price of a meal or a drink, please tell me you have uttered the words 'hooooow much?' when you last bought a drink! This will make you laugh, the office furniture people called to arrange delivery of all of my purchases the other day and I ended up adding another bookcase to the order! I seriously need to stop the furniture-buying obsession I seem to have developed! I am getting ready to go back to work, it is definitely time as I have started to turn into Delia Smith, I have lost count of the number of apple crumbles I churned out this week! The chutney however was a disaster, one batch came out like soup and the other like Tarmac!*
>
> *I continue to maintain that life is getting a little better every day, of course I miss Nick but I get what life will be like and it is not all bad. I sold some of Nick's vinyl records this week (he was an avid punk fan back in the day and they are quite collectible). I am glad as it's more money for the Cancer Research pot. I still haven't managed to consider clearing his wardrobe or bedside table, quite frankly I don't care if I never do, I suppose it's my way of hanging on.*

I so relate to your story of the Sunday breakdown, I lost count of the little things I found in Nick's office that made me howl. The receipt for my engagement ring that he had kept all these 15 years, the notebook where he had been writing his 'to do' list right at the end, so ill and still keeping focused on what needed doing to finish our dream kitchen (which we finished 10 days before he died).

Are you sleeping well? I ask because my sleep was absolutely awful for the first couple of months after Nick passed. I think it was partly because he slept very little in the last few weeks so I got out of the habit. But just the last couple of weeks I am starting to sleep much better, have become a little hooked to terrible late night tv though which doesn't help! I can't get enough of Brit Cops Abroad, Gypsy Sisters, the Magaluf Weekender or Toddlers & Tiaras.

It struck Kate, when reading this back several months later, that the writing was a stream of consciousness – a word-dump for everything that she happened to be feeling that night, with no real beginning or middle, and the end just left there in suspended animation. Who finishes a message with the words 'Toddlers & Tiaras'? She reflected that this was a very valuable insight into where she had been then – and also saw that the green shoots of recovery were already present in the message, which comforted her. She was also somewhat relieved that she had eventually managed to kick her furniture-buying habit, but not before she had managed to rack up three bookcases, one dining-room table with eight chairs, one new desk for the office, two filing cabinets, three chests of drawers, one enormous sideboard and two bedside tables!

Letter to Nick.

What on earth will I do with all of this Arsenal memorabilia? Cataloguing 331 back-copies of 'The Gooner' was not my idea of fun, but it's done so they just need a home now. I listened to some of your punk records before sending them off to a collector. Your early musical taste was certainly colourful! I think my favourite was taken from the lovely album by the Anti-Nowhere League. Such beautiful lyrics:

We are the League and we are mean.
We are the League and we're obscene.
Don't give a toss what you think.
And all your views they fucking stink.

It made me realise I wasn't being all that daring choosing a Pink Floyd track for your funeral after all!

Widow, 42
seeks furniture dealer. Strictly
for furniture purchases only.

Chapter 9

Those first few weeks back at work were packed full of reviewing CVs, interviewing and trying to rebuild the somewhat decimated remains of her team. In many ways Kate was a little relieved that so much change was happening at work, as it gave her the opportunity to start afresh with a largely new group of colleagues. She wouldn't have to remain stuck in the past, ruminating on what had happened with those members of her team who had lived through those fateful months with her.

Kate always found that interviews threw up some crazy situations, and this time was no different. There was the man who arrived an hour and a half after his allotted time and didn't even acknowledge that he was late. When asked what had brought him there that day he replied 'a car', with absolutely no hint of irony. There was the woman who had performed so well at her first interview, yet by the time Kate had invited her for a second interview together with her boss, seemed to have grown two heads and totally bombed. There were also the many occasions when Kate simply got bored during interviews and played her own games while 'listening' to the candidates giving their life histories. One of her favourite such games was 'Which bar of chocolate are you?' During those weeks she met a Double Decker (with not much up top), a KitKat (promising on the outside, but with wafer-thin substance), a Snickers (nutty, of course), a Curly Wurly (never thought she'd get to the end of it) and a selection box (didn't know what was coming next). However, three new recruits were eventually selected and the next thing she turned her mind to was how to convey her own back-story.

In the sales environment Kate worked in it was pretty normal to share quite specific details about one's life with colleagues – at least, Kate liked to. She felt this led to a greater sense of 'team', while fostering trust and friendship in the workplace. Being so recently widowed, Kate was still wondering how she would say, as matter-of-factly as possible, 'I'm widowed,' when meeting new people at work. She felt sure that this would elicit some sort of further questioning or response that she wasn't sure she could deal with. It turned out that she needn't have worried too much. She found it easier than anticipated and, like so many things, it got easier every time she said it. That was until she told one recruit, who promptly burst into tears. 'I wasn't expecting that,' thought Kate, as she comforted her new team-member.

Three short weeks after Kate returned to work there was a sales conference which the whole business unit was due to attend. This was one of Kate's early challenges: so many people who had known her for over ten years would be there, and would surely be feeling awkward themselves about seeing her again for the first time. What would they say to her? What would she reply? Not to mention the fact that she had gone away in May, not to be seen or heard of at all, before subsequently popping up again in September, fantastically tanned, considerably thinner and with braces on her teeth!

In addition Rachel, who had formerly been her 'rock' in the workplace, would not be there to hold her hand through this, as she had been the whole of the previous year. In a quirk of fate, their little team had been restructured only one short month before Nick had died, with the result that Rachel had been removed from Kate's day-to-day working life, which was a significant blow.

It turned out that the thought of the conference was more daunting than the actual event itself. Perhaps because the thought of it brought back such painful memories of the last such meeting she had been at – when the call from Emily had come through, telling her she was needed urgently at home because Nick had gone rapidly downhill. The times Kate had played that back in her mind, each time feeling so nauseous at the thought that maybe she should never have gone away in the first place. 'I robbed us of those last few days together,' Kate would tell herself over and over in her mind. Of course, her rational thoughts told her otherwise; but the gremlins would creep in and convince her that somehow, if she went back in time, things would have been different. It took conscious hard work every day during those first few months to fight those gremlins – but the fight was worth it, because they did scuttle back to where they came from, and remain there to this day.

Kate managed to get through all three days of the conference without tears or tantrums – at least, not in public. At the end of each day she caught herself several times about to call home to tell Nick an amusing story or just to 'check in', but then stopped herself short, realising there was no one to check in with any more. These were heart-breaking moments, as Kate had always enjoyed regaling Nick with the latest goings-on at work. Now, despite being surrounded by dozens of her colleagues, she felt absolutely alone.

Reflecting after the conference was over, however, Kate felt it had been like returning home to a huge family gathering. There had been friendly faces everywhere, people she had 'lost' during those three months away from work who had obviously been concerned for her, hugging, embracing, offering sympathies and support.

Kate had been eased gently back into work but now felt she needed to pick the reins up fully and start travelling, to spend time with her team across the southern half of the country. The train had become her preferred method of travel over the past couple of years, because long hours in the car would wear her down considerably. The route Kate had planned for her first trip was familiar: she would take the High Speed line to St Pancras, jump on the Tube to Paddington, and within a couple of hours she would be in Bristol. Of course, there were the times she simply couldn't face the Tube and would choose a black cab instead, which was always a roulette wheel of a journey, depending on the driver. There had been one occasion when her cab had actually crashed. The driver had leapt out for a fight with the other driver, not even bothering to check if Kate was Ok. The rest of that journey had been filled with her driver explaining that he didn't have an anger problem – which had made a normally fairly relaxed Kate pretty nervous on the whole.

This was a trip she must have done a hundred times or more, but absolutely nothing could have prepared her for the enormity of this apparently small step on her road back to working life. Kate disembarked from the train at St Pancras and allowed the crowd to surf her along the platform, as it always did in rush hour. This was a throng of tired-looking men in the main, some in sharp suits (obviously bankers) and others in plaster-covered jeans, carrying spirit levels, heading for the latest London development, where they would help to build the capital. As she reached the end of the escalator and walked outside into the September sunshine, both Kate's legs completely gave way.

She could not breathe. She staggered for a few seconds. She dropped her bag. She grabbed the nearby metal railing, clinging to it with such force that her knuckles turned white. The cold of the railing ran through her hands like pins, as she leaned her body forward and allowed it to take her full weight. Time seemed to stand still; Kate was trapped in an airless bubble while everything around her moved on painfully slowly. Gasping for air and desperately trying to regain feeling in her legs, she reached down to pick up her discarded bag. Huge teardrops blinded her and seemed to flood the pavement. She could not see to grab the bag and found herself aimlessly waving her hands around, hoping that she would make contact with the bag by accident, at least. A few nearby smokers glanced at her, but did nothing more than blow their smoke into the air and carry on chatting. This made Kate feel sick.

Having finally managed to regain the use of her legs, Kate gathered her things together and made her way across the road. To her left she saw people sitting outside a café enjoying coffee together and chatting. 'Why are they all bloody couples, looking deliriously happy?' thought Kate. 'That's just cruel.' Words went round and round in her head with every single step of the walk between stations. 'Their whole lives ahead of them... A shared life, a happy life, *a life*.' She was still half-blinded by tears and so choked she felt like she had swallowed a tennis ball. 'Why am I even here?' This was a common question that she had pondered often during the last three months. There was the existential question of why any of us are here and what purpose we serve; but also the practical question in Kate's mind about whether work was what she wanted out of life any more. She had seriously considered whether to throw everything in the air and jump off the roundabout of life completely. This would often make her think of Philip Larkin, her favourite poet, and his lines from 'Poetry of Departures'.

> Sometimes you hear, fifth-hand,
> As epitaph:
> He chucked up everything
> And just cleared off,
> And always the voice will sound
> Certain you approve
> This audacious, purifying,
> Elemental move.

However, so often the sensible part of her mind had reasoned with this notion and convinced her that decisions made in haste and at times of crisis could be long-regretted.

Kate realised she was wandering aimlessly around King's Cross station, having walked right past the entrance to the Underground. With mascara running down her cheeks and looking like a dishevelled, unhappy wreck, someone took pity on her and asked if she needed help. This was a surprise to Kate. It was her theory that anyone commuting in London had been stripped of their human faculties and had become cyber-men, prepared to kill or maim in order to reach their destination faster. It was also alarming for Kate, as she had come to realise that there was nothing more likely to evoke an extreme emotional response than the kindness of strangers. 'Oh no – here comes the snot-snort,' she thought, as she tried to reply to the kindly stranger. 'Game over.'

<u>Letter to Nick.</u>

I would sell everything I own and live on the streets for just one more day with you. The emptiness of the situation hit me harder today than a train.

Widow, 42
seeks the warmth and
friendship of work colleagues.

Chapter 10

More 'firsts' were heading Kate's way. She could see them looming on the horizon with menacing clarity and she simply did not know how she would react when they arrived. First anniversary; first Christmas; first birthday without him. If her 'first trip through King's Cross' experience was anything to go by, Kate didn't rate her chances of successfully navigating these 'firsts' unscathed.

'Come on, Kate, you're better than that!' she told herself. 'Descending into a self-pitying succession of firsts that throw you off course? Not bloody likely!'

She laughed out loud as she thought of the time that she and Nick had managed to manufacture a blazing row out of a comment he had made. 'I reckon you've lost the edge,' Nick had said, deliberately trying to provoke her. She had reacted, of course, and from that day till now had always been mindful of the fact that 'more chilled' did not equate to 'lost the edge'. This thought pulled her out of lacklustre feelings of hopelessness whenever they invaded her space.

The Shine London charity walk that Kate, Clare and Lou had signed up for was only three weeks away, so she decided the best thing she could do was focus heavily on that. Training had been fairly regular, but not exactly stretching, so they really needed to up their game. The walk was to take place at night around the streets of London, with participants advised to wear neon colours so that they would all 'Shine' in the dark. They had opted for the half-marathon as opposed to the full marathon and the nearer the event drew, the happier Kate was about this choice. After all, just three months before, the only serious miles she had walked were around Bluewater or Lakeside shopping centres.

While physically preparing for the big day, Kate had also been taking care to continue her counselling with Audrey, in order to ensure that she was mentally strong enough. After that somewhat quirky first counselling session, Kate had come to look forward to their bi-weekly chats. Somehow they cleared a little space in her mind, which allowed free-flowing thought to break through from time to time. It was as though Kate's brain had shut down every compartment except for those deemed absolutely essential for living and breathing. Reopening some of the closed compartments brought immense relief for Kate; it meant that there might just be the possibility of 'normal' one day returning.

By this time Kate had moved beyond talking about guilt and utter despair and was now acknowledging that she was downright scared to stop talking and thinking about Nick all the time, just in case the memory faded. Audrey reassured her that it was perfectly Ok to talk to photos of Nick, Ok to talk out loud in the house, and even Ok to talk to the cats. She seemed to find it interesting that Kate had stopped having dreams, so they spent time discussing what the impact of this might be and why. Kate had always been a prolific dreamer – sometimes her nights were so packed with dreams that she would wake the next morning feeling exhausted. So vivid were some of her dreams that they had an impact on her waking hours, especially the recurring one about choking on chewing-gum. Over the years she must have had this dream in various guises more than a thousand times and the build-up over the years had eventually led her to eschew all gum for ever. The start was always the same: while Kate was trying to talk intently to someone, the gum would be expanding like foam in her mouth. She would surreptitiously turn away from the person she was speaking to, trying to claw the gum out of her mouth, but as she did so it kept on expanding. Despite the previous frequency of this and other dreams, from the day of Nick's death Kate had completely stopped dreaming. She figured it must be another compartment of her brain which had been closed down due to lack of space. She often felt this was a great shame during those early months, as she believed she would have derived some comfort in seeing Nick again, even if it were in dream-form.

Others had their own theories about Kate's lack of dreams. One such theory was that Nick was deliberately staying away so as not to scare Kate. A notorious scaredy-cat when it came to the supernatural – or, at the very least, the unexplained – Kate agreed that this would be the sort of thoughtful action Nick would take. However, there was the nagging fact that Kate simply did not believe in life after death and therefore could not in all consciousness subscribe to this theory. Believing in the 'unexplained' was as far as Kate could go on this, although she had yearned throughout her life to date, and none less now, for some evidence that people dead and alive could meet on an astral plain through dreams. Why else would some random person from twenty years ago suddenly pop up in dreams for no apparent reason?

Kate told Audrey how she was acutely aware that every time she conversed with anybody, somehow she would find a way to manufacture the conversation back to something Nick had said or done in the past – as though all roads now led to Nick, no matter where they started or where they were originally going. Audrey assured her that this was understandable and a healthy way to stay in touch, but Kate worried that people were going to start doing one of three things: become bored of anecdotes about Nick – ones they had probably heard before, or even lived through the first time around; start changing the conversation to avoid 'Nick chat'; or, worst of all, stop wanting to spend time with her altogether! Ultimately Kate had no control over this anyway, so she decided that whatever would be, would be. She often took comfort in some words that a very new but surprisingly good friend had written to her a few days after Nick's death: 'Be kind to yourself, do whatever you want to do, whenever you want to do it.' Even if living to this mantra would eventually create a monster, it surely was a good philosophy in those early days.

The day of the charity walk arrived – bright and sunny, with unusually high temperatures forecast for a mid-autumn evening. Their preparation in the last week had been more focused on what they would wear. Kate, Lou and Clare proudly sported their official blue T-shirts, paired with as many neon accessories as they could find. These included some ridiculous oversized bows for their hair which made each of them look like a slightly manic Minnie Mouse. They were not used to travelling in London on a Saturday afternoon, and were amazed at how busy it was. There were hordes of football supporters travelling to and from games, singing, drinking and generally jostling on the Tube carriages. Amongst them, in not inconsiderable numbers, were also large groups of people off to the charity walk – all in the uniform of trainers and blue T-shirts with 'Shine' emblazoned across the chest. It gave Kate a sense of belonging – a sense she found exhilarating and energising, which was just what she needed at that point.

At the starting-point in Southwark Park, Kate, Lou and Clare started to sense the scale of the event. There was a huge stage at the front of the park, flanked on either side by banners, balloons, lasers and stalls. Walkers were arriving in endless waves, piling through the wrought-iron gates of the park, chattering excitedly and collecting their numbers and glo-sticks. Everyone was issued with flashing wristbands – the organisers were determined to light up the London streets that night, and it felt to Kate as though she was really part of something very special. As the light started to fade and the music blasted from the stage, the atmosphere in the park began to electrify and there was a real air of anticipation. Thousands of people crowded forwards, moving nearer to the stage as Mr Motivator started the fun warm-up routine. Kate estimated that Mr Motivator, clad head-to-foot in lycra, must be at least sixty years old, but he had not lost his verve and he easily whipped the expectant crowd into a frenzy of dance moves in a bid to warm everyone up both physically and mentally. Inevitably, as the crowd stepped left, Kate stepped right; and as everyone skipped forwards,

Kate skipped backwards. But this didn't matter – she was actually having fun. Kate, Lou and Clare laughed along with the rest of the crowd, looking forward to the challenge ahead.

Eventually the moment arrived when their group was called forward to the start. The three of them had elected to join the medium-paced group, knowing that they were not the fittest or the fastest walkers, but also – they assumed – not the slowest. However, it looked like every single participant had made the same decision. Thousands of people lined up along the starting funnel, which seemed to stretch at least a mile ahead of them. The walk through that starting section felt like it took for ever; it was painfully slow, due to the sheer numbers of bodies crowded into the area. Nevertheless there was a feeling of great camaraderie and it gave all three of them a chance to see the impressive diversity of people who had taken on this challenge. The organisers had issued all walkers with A4-sized 'I'm walking in memory of…' labels to attach to the backs of their blue T-shirts. Kate had written simply 'Nick' on hers – she couldn't bring herself to write anything more than that. Lou had written the name of her much-missed uncle and, being artistic, had drawn some little hearts and flowers. Looking around her, Kate was struck by the heart-wrenching messages people had written – thousands of people walking in memory of the tens of thousands of people they had lost. So many remembering 'Granny' or 'Grandad'; too many remembering 'Mum' or 'Dad'; and a smattering remembering 'My dear sister' or 'My much missed brother'. Without doubt the saddest one of all was a lone woman in her thirties whose label simply read: 'For my son Tommy.'

Having taken the best part of an hour to actually make it through the start, the three friends decided they needed to make up time and marched, as best they could, through the crowds towards the leading pack. After a short distance they passed the Tower of London, which had been festooned that year with hundreds of thousands of ceramic poppies in memory of those who had died in service during the First World War. Kate, Lou and Clare allowed themselves a couple of minutes to take in the carpet of red flowers, lit up at ground level and with the stern backdrop of the Tower looming over them. It was a stunning sight and with emotions running high that night already, it brought a lump to Kate's throat.

Another mile along the route, the three friends decided it was high time for a burst of sugar. Disregarding things like water or blister plasters, the only 'essentials' any of them had packed were sweets and at this stage, two and a half hours in, a cola cube was a very welcome distraction. The crowds were starting to thin out by then, as everyone found their own walking pace and, inevitably, each new mile saw a few more people sitting on the edge of the pavement nursing sore feet and applying plasters. It wasn't long before the three of them agreed that, with hindsight, they should have put less effort into the Mr Motivator warm-up and saved more energy for this inescapable eleven o'clock low-point.

'I need a wee,' announced Clare, as they passed Buckingham Palace at about midnight.

'Me too,' the other two piped up. As they hadn't seen a Portaloo for ages, they decided to stop at Victoria station – where they found that the toilets cost thirty pence each to use.

'Bloody cheek!' said Lou, as she skipped over the barrier to avoid the charge. After ten miles of walking, Kate and Clare were not feeling as spritely. In attempting the same manoeuvre as Lou, Kate managed to hook her T-shirt onto the revolving barrier, nearly strangling herself in the process. Whether caused by the sugar overload from all the sweets, or hysteria brought on by fatigue, the three of them collapsed into a laughing heap just beyond the barriers, unable to move for a moment.

The rest of the walk passed steadily and uneventfully, apart from the occasional announcement from each of them about which part of her body hurt the most. Thirteen miles came and went according to Clare's app, but they were still at least half a mile from the finish line.

'Well, they lied about the distance,' Clare complained. All Kate could manage in response was a woeful nod.

The finish itself was, by contrast, a joyous affair – a mixture of relief and delight in being given finishers' medals. Kate was amused by how excited people could get over a small piece of plastic tied to a length of blue ribbon; but looking back at the finishers' photo of them holding up their medals and beaming, she concluded that they were genuinely delighted at what they had achieved.

Letter to Nick.

I walked 13 miles in memory of you today. It brought you closer but it didn't bring you back.

Widow, 42
seeks the companionship
and camaraderie of
thousands of strangers.

Chapter 11

Thanks to the now-overused mantra of 'Nick would have wanted me to', Kate had booked a luxury holiday that autumn. With her mother and Emily always ready and willing to sign up to a holiday, this was not the hardest thing they had agreed to do in support of Kate in recent months. By this time they had successfully negotiated the scattering of Nick's ashes, while as a permanent memorial Kate had decided on a bench for the garden, with the inscription: 'Better to burn out than to fade away.' She felt sure that Nick would have approved of something less lame than 'Rest in peace' – and she could just imagine what he would have said to something like 'Sweetly sleeping'! With these accomplishments behind them, a luxury holiday seemed very justifiable.

The hotel they had settled on, in Gran Canaria, looked palatial. The weather promised a balmy twenty-five degrees by day and the hotel was right by the seaside, with cocktail bars a-plenty and an excellent selection of pools to choose from. The photos on the website looked amazing and the reviews could say no wrong about the place, so the decision had been made: they were off to soak up some autumn sun.

By the time of the holiday, Kate had been back at work for seven weeks. This actually only equated to twenty-two days of work, because she had agreed a phased return, designed to ease her back gradually into the rigours of a *very* full-time job. The usual excitement of a sunny holiday was tempered by uncertainty on Kate's part about how she would really feel about going abroad for the first time without Nick.

As she stepped from the plane at Las Palmas, the familiar smell and feel of warm evening air was the reassurance Kate needed that she was doing the right thing. It was not that Kate had previously lacked confidence or independence, but that now every single decision was hers and hers alone – which required more energy than she had anticipated. Every once in a while she would have liked to leave one choice, however small or large, to someone else. Later she would find herself unable to make small decisions, like which sandwich filling to have, because, she thought, she had used up all of her 'choosing energy' when making the big decisions. The warm Canarian air swirled around her as she walked down the steps from the plane. She liked that feeling, having left England in the throes of autumn with its shorter days and colder nights.

Having navigated their way through passport control – where even one man in a small box seemed more efficient than Gatwick's state-of-the-art but incredibly slow system – and found their transfer bus, the journey time to their hotel was only another twenty minutes. Even though they had gone all-out for luxury, none of them was prepared for the sheer opulence of the hotel they had booked. As the porters rushed to take their bags on arrival, Kate felt a huge wave of relief wash over her – somehow this one act told her that she was no longer 'alone', doing everything for herself. Relief soon turned to awe as the grand architecture of the hotel opened in front of her. They stared, open-mouthed, at the infinity pool, which was lit up like the fountains at the Palace of Versailles. 'Infinity' of course implies 'for ever', but rarely did that actually seem to apply to such pools, Kate thought, as she announced to the others: 'This really does go on for ever... and ever!'

The three of them stood and stared as though they were looking at the Seventh Wonder of the World. This break was going to be a good one.

The next morning it was time to explore. The hotel offered a spectacular choice of delights, including every conceivable type of pool – one for every possible mood or need. First there was the chill-out pool at the far end of the hotel. Oblong and lined on all sides by stone dogs, each spouting a soothing trickle of water into the pool throughout the day, the chill-out pool was largely frequented by people over fifty and had a strictly-enforced 'no inflatables' policy. The palm trees surrounding this pool offered natural shade and the nearby pool-bar was sumptuously furnished with reclining chairs and offered the most delicious fresh fruit smoothies Kate had ever tasted. 'It would be so easy to stay fit and healthy here,' thought Kate, unrealistically. 'I would swim several times a day and live off smoothies.' This pool was where total relaxation existed and several books could be read; for pure, unadulterated introspection.

Later in the morning they also sampled that incredible infinity pool, the jewel around which the whole hotel had been built. Stretching from a marvellous open terrace – housing all sorts of little restaurants and the impressive cocktail bar which had already caught their eye – to the wide blue swathe of the Atlantic, this pool offered serious swimmers the opportunity to lose themselves for a while. Kate counted how many strokes it took to swim end-to-end. Depending on how vigorously she attempted it, the average was a whopping 125! It was the coldest of the pools, purely as a result of the sheer amount of water it contained, but the temperatures by day and night were more than ample to allow for this, so Kate concluded that it did not detract from the experience one little bit.

Just when Kate, Emily and their mother thought these two pools couldn't be topped, they found the lazy river pool. This was a narrow pool that snaked its way around much of the hotel grounds with a little current continuously pushing swimmers along. Now and then it would open up into small coves, with waterfalls cascading down to offer swimmers a refreshing shower of water. This pool was best for a relaxing swim or a ride on an inflatable. The more decadent holiday-makers combined a ride on a lilo with a drink in-hand. Where the first pool felt like the Sea of Tranquillity and the second felt like the Never-Ending Story, the lazy river offered Kate the most carefree fun she had felt in a long time.

Adjoining the lazy river was the exercise pool, where everything from water polo to aqua aerobics took place throughout the day. A lively beach-bar blared out music when an activity was about to start and Panchi would regularly turn up unannounced to drive the kids crazy with delight. Panchi was a new and strangely annoying concept to Kate and her family. Although obviously very popular among the children staying at the hotel, the draw of the five-foot-tall blue dolphin would remain a mystery to them throughout their holiday. Emily actually threatened to push him into the water one day, when he arrived unannounced and stood in her precious sun-spot. Kate was pretty sure that he would have drowned if Emily had carried out her threat, as the dolphin costume looked cumbersome and unlikely to aid swimming.

There was also a giant Jacuzzi with views over the harbour – the perfect place to watch the sun set each evening – and even a saltwater flotation tank. The tank was an amazing experience underground in the spa (they had treated themselves again). The peace was only shattered when Kate accidentally licked her lips while floating, and swallowed what she guessed was at least a year's worth of salt. Much choking ensued, and she was asked to leave the area in order to restore the tranquillity of the cave-like surroundings.

So the pools ticked all possible boxes, no matter what mood anyone was in. Kate felt good about this holiday; it was just what she needed at this pivotal time. After all, she had survived those crucial first three months, clinging on to her sense of being as firmly as she could. While everything around her seemed to slip and slide into uncertainty, she had kept listening to that inner voice, the one which assured her that there *would* be a time when some good would emerge from all the chaos she felt. It was better to believe in something than nothing. Why did Kate listen to that voice? Because if she didn't, she would have had to listen to the voice which told her she had let Nick down just when he needed her most. She knew that other voice spoke a lie, one sent to derail her, and she felt lucky that she had been so stubborn in resolutely refusing to listen to it.

The holiday had also been strategically placed at just the right time from a work perspective. After seven weeks back in her job she was already feeling the need for a break, both mentally and physically. Kate was amazed by how quickly work could wear her down, something she had never fully understood before, having rarely taken more than a week off at a time. Three months off, therefore, had taught her to slow down. The need to speed up again had been taxing, not least because she was still not sleeping many hours each night. As she sat contemplating all of this on the beautiful terrace that first full evening in their hotel, she felt a massive pang of guilt. She would never have been able to afford a holiday like this if Nick had still been around. She sipped her mojito and looked down over the palm-lined path which led out to the beach beyond. 'I've paid too high a price for all of this,' she sighed to herself.

Then her mother and Emily arrived, chattering excitedly about the hotel, the cocktails, the pools… All this helped distract Kate from her inner thoughts – the ones she dared not share with anyone other than Audrey the counsellor. She dared not share them as she didn't want anyone to feel they had to say, 'Of course you didn't let him down.' Or worse still, to tell her, 'It doesn't work like that – bad things can just happen to good people, and Nick was the best.'

So they ordered more cocktails and Emily instigated her standard holiday conversation: 'How long do you reckon we could all live in this hotel if we sold everything and moved in permanently?'

Their mother worked out that she could probably see her days out, and the three of them were just laughing and doing the maths on how long Emily could stay when a clown popped up from behind the rattan sofa they were all sitting on.

'Not joining in?' he asked. It seemed that some sort of entertainment was happening in the far corner of the terrace.

Kate could not respond, as she was frozen with fear and indignant at the interruption in equal measure. Anyone who knew Kate would know that top of her list of 'dislikes' were clowns, who in her mind were insidious creatures having no valid place in any form of entertainment or, in fact, any occasion. This simply made the whole incident even funnier for Emily and their mother, who were rendered speechless by laughter. The poor old clown slinked off, his jolly persona very much dented.

'You've pulled a clown!' joked Emily.

'The nerve of him,' grumbled Kate.

Letter to Nick.

We scattered your ashes in the garden on our wedding anniversary. It was a windy day and most of them ended up on Dad's shoes – he says he will never bring himself to clean them again!

Widow, 42
seeks anything but the
company of clowns.

Chapter 12

Gran Canaria could not have provided more rest and relaxation for the three bereavement-weary travellers. A cruise along the coast offered a further change of scene and the chance to see some of the dolphins and whales which frequented the waters around the island. They had decided on a half-day aboard the magnificent-looking *Aphrodite*, a traditional sailing-boat which, in the holiday literature they had read, looked proud to sail the waters. The additional promise of sangria and prosecco had sealed the deal. Taking the short bus journey to the port of Puerto Rico, Kate reminisced about the many trips she and Nick had taken. They had loved to travel and had certainly not wasted time in that respect, taking every opportunity that reared its head to go somewhere, anywhere. Quite often her mother and Emily would be in tow; looking back, Kate reflected on how tolerant Nick had been about that. In fact, he had even managed to find the strength the day before his death to recount the story of *that* holiday in Rhodes for their friend Julie's wedding. Wracked with pain and barely able to whisper by then, he had taken the time to entertain his audience (Kate, her brother and her sister-in-law) by describing how Kate and Emily had ended up with food poisoning, meaning he had found himself traipsing round Rhodes town looking for anti-sickness medication; then, in desperation, as they still hadn't recovered by the second day, he had spent the whole day on the beach with Mum!

As the bus arrived in Puerto Rico, the three of them agreed about how glad they were that they had chosen a smaller, quieter resort for their stay. A typically bustling port and harbour, Puerto Rico did not lack charm but it did have more than its fair share of the tourist population per square foot. Despite the fact that Kate was not a confident sea-goer, she always found a harbour – with its range of vessels, from tiny wooden fishing-boats to huge yachts dripping with the trimmings of wealth – a romantic sight. Somehow it conjured up visions of new beginnings, romantic trysts and the idea that one could just sail away if it all went wrong. She could not pinpoint why she felt this way, as her only real-life experiences of harbours had involved short cruises or cups of tea. Nevertheless the feeling was there, which meant another point to tick off on Kate's list of things to achieve on holiday – 'to really start to feel again,' as she put it.

The cruise was a great hit with all three of them: pure relaxation plus a dash of excitement when they not only saw dolphins for the first time but had them swim alongside the boat for several minutes. Not long after that, Kate pointed out to the horizon.

'What's that?' she asked, just as the boat turned sharply. Clearly, whatever she had seen had also been spotted by the crew, as they powered ahead to the new object of interest in the water.

As they drew near another passenger yelled: 'A whale!'

Shrieks of excitement followed – sure enough, it really was a whale. As they all watched it surface for air, blowing a jet of water, Kate found herself shouting, 'Wow… So big!'

One of the crew announced, 'And that's the baby, so we should see the mama soon!' While all this was happening they had been enjoying a sumptuous lunch. With the delicious food, the moreish sangria and the amazing marine life, Kate felt the chance to start letting go at last.

Kate had always had a terrible habit of nicknaming people, even strangers. Sometimes it would be because of the person's look or character; or sometimes just because they resembled someone famous. There had been The Grimmers, who had lived down the road from her several years back, a noisy family who seemed to take no pride in their appearance or that of their house. Meanwhile Nosey Old Bird used to walk past Kate's house several times a day, purely in order to stare in, it seemed. Nosey Old Bird would even offer to walk other people's dogs, having none of her own, for this same purpose. One such dog was Scooby-Doo, who lived at the end of the road. That wasn't his actual name but he was – according to Kate, at least – the spitting image of the cartoon character, and he carried a sad story which Kate found interesting. According to local legend he had run into an old lady and, as he was so big, he had broken both her legs, ultimately leading to her demise. This came into sharp focus the day he had escaped from his house and ended up running down Kate's driveway. She had run out to catch him, shouting 'Scooby!' – at which point he had turned and started bolting directly towards her. Recalling the legend of the old lady who had died of the broken legs, Kate had started running rapidly backwards, shouting 'Slow down Scooby, slow down!' As she had hit the garage door with her back, he had mercifully slowed down and trotted up to her calmly. Kate's relief had been visible, not least to her next-door neighbour, who had witnessed the whole thing from her kitchen window and was laughing unashamedly.

Several lookie-likies had already cropped up on their holiday so far, but none so impressive as the Canarian Philip Schofield, who they met in a steak restaurant one night. Overlooking the sea to the front of the verandah, and the impressive hotel grounds to the side, there was no such thing as a bad view from anywhere in the restaurant. But because Philip Schofield had taken an instant liking to Emily, they were offered the very best table in the house, the 'Reserved' label quickly swiped away as they sat down. 'Wow,' thought Kate. 'That has never happened to me before!' A little pang of jealousy hit a nerve somewhere deep in her chest. Emily had the ability to turn heads in a way Kate could only dream of – and the crazy thing was that Emily didn't even know it.

Later that evening, as the three sat finishing their superb meal, the Canarian Philip Schofield could not resist his amorous inclinations any longer. He declared to their mother: 'You have such a beautiful daughter.'

This made their mother laugh, Emily blush and Kate just grumble, '*Two* beautiful daughters,' which fell on deaf ears. As they were leaving, to the words of Philip declaring his undying love for Emily, Kate announced: 'If the food hadn't been so bloody good I'd never go back!'

Kate's return to England after that spectacular holiday was destined to be a bit of a crash-landing, back to the harsh reality of her new, somewhat solitary, life. It was not that she lacked great friends or family – it was simply the fact that she was now living alone for the first time ever, which was taking some getting used to. It was mainly the lack of noise that disconcerted Kate, so much so, that almost every room would have to have a radio playing or a TV on. Of course, she would talk to the cats every day, and never walked past a photo of Nick without pausing to touch it or talk to him. This period was the countdown to another inevitable 'first': in early November the prospect of that first Christmas without Nick was looming. Prior to her holiday Kate had decided to continue renovations to the house, which meant that work started the day she arrived home. She had thought that overseeing this would be a good distraction for her – and in many ways she was right. However, on several occasions throughout the run-up to Christmas she wondered why she always had to pack things into the most inopportune moments, thereby putting herself under maximum pressure.

The project had started as a simple task to 'finish off the downstairs' – but by the time Kate had fully scoped out the job, it had grown to include a bespoke staircase (just like the one Nick had liked so much in those fancy brochures he had ordered, but at a fraction of the cost) and a complete remodelling of the two remaining upstairs bedrooms. Luckily, the master bedroom had been completed the previous year, just before Nick's diagnosis, which at least meant that he had had pleasant surroundings in which to endure the devastatingly cruel after-effects of his punishing treatment.

First things first: Fit Plumber needed to come and work out the complicated mass of pipes in the back bedroom, which was laughingly called 'the office'. Both Nick and Kate had worked from home, so they had shared this space, which was ample but muddled, to say the least. All of Nick's work things had been removed, but in their place were the piles of papers that came with someone's death. Bank statements, insurance claims, pension forms, ISA documents, tax records; and the trio of birth, marriage and death certificates. Kate had worked hard to clear all this, but even harder to remove the rows and rows of shelving with which her grandfather had covered every inch of one whole wall. In typical Grandad style, the shelving had been nailed, glued *and* screwed – so inevitably it came away with half the wall attached. This was when Kate had the inspiration to knock a new window into the wall. 'I might as bloody well,' she had thought to herself while removing the last of the shelving. 'I'm practically through to the other side now anyway.' So the project grew again: 'Angle-grinding a new window into this wall – I am truly a project manager and architect in one!' she proclaimed.

After Fit Plumber arrived there was much scratching of heads to work out why on earth there were quite so many pipes in the room. They concluded that it must have been one of her grandfather's creative ideas to keep his feet warm. 'Bloody ugly and definitely coming out,' they both agreed.

Fit Plumber had become quite a friend to Kate over the months following that first, terribly awkward, meeting. If not a friend, then certainly someone she could depend upon and someone who understood how much the house meant to her. He would often jokingly ask, 'When are you going to sell this place to me?' He seemed to love it almost as much as she did. Fit Plumber grew to understand the quirky pipework and knew always to expect the unexpected when he arrived for a job. There was the time he arrived just in time to find Kate and her friend Nicky shrieking and chasing a baby rabbit around the living-room – one of the many gifts which the dear cats brought in. Or the time he arrived to find Kate hiding from the Southern Water lady, who had come to talk about installing a water meter – which, with all those fields and water troughs to fill, would have been disastrous.

Fit Plumber was easy to talk to, an especially nice trait for Kate, who sometimes craved 'man-talk'. He liked to talk about kit cars, motor sport, stag-dos and the like, the sorts of things that Kate would have listened to Nick talk about, not realising at the time how much she would miss them. One night Kate had kept Fit Plumber chatting so long that he finally left at nearly ten o'clock, despite having finished his work by seven. 'Oh gosh, Kate…' she said to herself as he left, 'you really are needy!'

Letter to Nick.

I put all of your treasures into a box today and as the lid went on I felt so guilty that I was locking you away. It was so hard to choose which treasures would make the cut – how do you fit someone's 48 years into a 40 cm × 30 cm box?

Widow, 42
seeks plush holidays in
the name of 'healing'.

Chapter 13

To everyone around her Kate seemed to be coping well in the run-up to Christmas. Despite living in the dusty surroundings of a partial building-site, she organised Christmas lunches and evenings out, and once the builders finally left on 14 December she scurried around putting up decorations as though nothing had happened.

One of her close friends even remarked: 'You know, Kate, you're grieving in style.'

This made Kate proud and sad all at once. 'I'm not waving but drowning,' she thought, following which she looked out her favourite Stevie Smith poem.

> Nobody heard him, the dead man,
> But still he lay moaning:
> I was much further out than you thought
> And not waving but drowning.
>
> Poor chap, he always loved larking
> And now he's dead
> It must have been too cold for him his heart
> gave way,
> They said.
>
> Oh, no no no, it was too cold always
> (Still the dead one lay moaning)
> I was much too far out all my life
> And not waving but drowning.

Emily had decided to throw a lavish Christmas party in honour of her own birthday, which, inconveniently for everyone, fell on 21 December. It was a risky idea: the drop-out rate for such events so close to Christmas was notoriously high. However, everyone had committed to make a huge effort not only to show up, but also to go full fancy-dress. Even Rachel, Kate's dear friend and 'rock' from work, had agreed to drive all the way from her home in Yorkshire for the occasion. The planning seemed never-ending but even Kate had to admit on the day of the party that it had been well worth all the effort.

The huge ramshackle barn that Emily had commandeered as her venue had been transformed by a mixture of creativity and sheer hard work – this was Emily's forte, creating fantasy worlds which were nothing like her own life.

Twenty artificial Christmas trees lined the 'snow-globe' entrance to the barn. Dusted in snow spray and twinkling with fairy lights, the effect was as magical as intended. When they stepped through the doorway of the barn, the party-goers were transported into a silvery winter wonderland: soft white fabrics draped extravagantly from walls and ceiling; fake fur throws atop stools; glittering snowflakes lovingly painted on windows. The effect was skilfully topped off with a giant silver throne in one corner – great for fun photo opportunities, and a masterclass in how to create an incredibly effective look with an old chair, silver foil, twigs and a healthy number of cans of white and silver spray! Kate reckoned that the chair had probably come from one of their grandparents' houses when they were cleared some years ago.

In the adjoining room Emily had created a German Christmas market scene. In one corner stood a market stall, decked with holly garlands, fairy lights and red bows, offering a feast of Christmas treats, from gingerbread men to mulled wine. 'What an ingenious use of the slow cooker,' thought Kate as she helped herself to some of the wine. 'A much better use for it than boring old stew.' The market room was festooned with swathes of red and green fabric, and hundreds of candy canes thoughtfully hanging from the ceiling for peckish party-goers to pluck and eat at their leisure.

Kate chuckled as she noted the recycling Emily had accomplished with Fred the Zombie. Fred had arrived amongst much excitement just over a year earlier, when Emily had decided to throw the Halloween party to end all Halloween parties. Despite the fact that the whole party had been 'dressed' and executed with Emily's usual attention to detail, the centrepiece had definitely been Fred – the animatronic, life-size zombie that she had shipped from the USA with great extravagance. 'Bloody hell, what on earth did you pay for him?' Kate had asked at the time, but she had received no answer. 'How can we even be related?' Kate had continued to herself, wondering how one sister could be so frugal with spending while the other was only ever happy when spending money on the most frivolous and fun things in the world. The best thing about Fred had been when Emily had set him up in the spare room at their mother's house and scared the life out of the cleaner. The worst was when Emily had done exactly the same to Kate one night. This year Fred had received a makeover for the Christmas party, welcoming guests to Santa's Grotto resplendent in full Father Christmas suit, beard and glasses. Kate felt sure that no one would ever have guessed his grizzly past.

Fancy dress was the order of the day and every single guest made a great effort not to disappoint. There was the usual smattering of Sexy Santas – not least Rachel, who was the sexiest of Sexy Santas – dressed, it seemed, exclusively by Ann Summers! Looking back the next morning, Kate couldn't help laughing out loud at the flashback to Rachel dressed as Sexy Santa being happily chatted up by Jesus (the adult version, of course). Elves were also in abundance and in fact Kate had opted to attend as an elf, much to everyone's amusement, as this particular look seemed to suit her very well. Mum had outdone herself yet again in her sheer ability for randomness by coming as Rudolph, but not just with some cute antlers and a red nose – she had the full reindeer suit, complete with hooves and everything. Cousin Emma pulled off a very chic 'ice queen' look and had dressed her two-year-old daughter as a gingerbread man – not to her daughter's liking, being a major Disney princess fan. There was a superb nutcracker soldier costume; and a fully decorated, walking Christmas tree, complete with battery-operated lights. But the outfit that stole the show for Kate was the shepherd. 'Ingenious!' Kate exclaimed as Luke walked in. Dressed in a brown, threadbare charity-shop dressing gown, with rope tied round his waist, the look was completed by some very authentic-looking sandals and, of course, a tea-towel on his head. With a big stick (that he had found on the way to the party) in one hand and a blow-up sheep in the other, this was the costume to beat!

Kate always found that costume parties were somehow quick to get going. People seemed to leave their inhibitions at home with their normal day-to-day look, in favour of a more carefree and eccentric way of looking and acting. The party was soon in full swing, and Kate felt happy for her sister that so many people had come and made such an effort to dress up. The usual drinking games were quick to start; despite resolving not to overdo things that night, Kate found herself drawn into the world of beer pong and flip cup. As matters became ever more competitive, Kate realised that there was one of Emily's friends who she only ever saw at parties, and who specifically always seemed to be on the opposing team during drinking games. As Kate stood at the end of the beer pong table, ball in hand facing the opposition, here he was again, but this time dressed as an elf. So: this was *Elf v Elf* in the final of beer pong, with everything to play for. Several rounds had passed with no losers, which meant that by now the 'dirty pint' at the centre of the game was pretty dirty indeed. Both elves realised that the after-effects of drinking it might well reach into the new year for the unlucky loser. As Kate squared herself to the table and prepared to serve the ping pong ball towards the other end, she sized up her opposition. He looked like a sort of 'dark elf', as for some reason by this stage of the night he had acquired a fake stick-on 'monobrow' straddling his eyebrows. Perhaps it had been the nutcracker soldier's moustache? 'How on earth did that get there?' wondered Kate vaguely, giggling as she served.

Letter to Nick.

Oh how you used to love Em's parties and this one would have been no exception. You could party with the best of them – we found ourselves reminiscing during the evening about the scrapes you got into at some of those parties and the pranks you instigated. Like the time everyone was convinced you had killed yourself skateboarding down Corinne's mountainous garden at the now-infamous New Year's Eve party. Hitting the small wall at the bottom of the slope and launching yourself several feet into the air, no one waited to see you land on the patio below – they all just ran in shouting, 'Kate, Kate, Nick's killed himself!' We all ran out just in time to find you dusting yourself off, skateboard under one arm, pint of a strange green drink in your other hand and walking up the garden for another go.

We toasted absent friends at Em's party and even Aunty Sara played the traditional drinking games in your honour – we remember you and we miss you.

> **Widow, 42**
> seeks hangover cure
> because this night will
> surely end in Hangover City.

Chapter 14

22 December was a hard day for everyone. The mulled wine and dirty pints were fighting back after the night before, and the harsh reality of the sheer amount of clearing-up was just too much for anyone to cope with. So they shut the door to the barn, resolving to come back to it at a more convenient time – which actually arrived more than a year later.

While recalling the dance moves, the drinking games and the Christmas fairy who fell backwards off her chair at one point, showing everyone what fairies wear under their tutus, Kate remembered a conversation she had been having with Rachel and some other work friends.

'Bloody hell!' she suddenly blurted out, halfway through the Survivors' Breakfast. 'I signed up for some hike last night, didn't I?'

'The Yorkshire Three Peaks Challenge, to be precise,' answered Rachel – rather too gleefully, in Kate's opinion. 'I'm so glad you're doing it. It'll be great!'

'You didn't just sign *yourself* up,' chipped in Emily, shovelling baked beans into her mouth. She was looking less magical ice princess than the night before, and more dishevelled zombie. 'We've got twenty-six miles and three mountains to do in May… Thanks for that!'

'Shit,' was all Kate could muster before returning to her bacon butty.

The more Kate thought about it as the day went on, though, the more she realised it was just the sort of challenge she needed to give her focus for the year ahead. The Shine walk they had done in the autumn had been a truly uplifting experience, so why shouldn't this next challenge be just the same? Granted, Shine had been thirteen miles around the flat streets of London, whereas this new challenge involved twice the distance plus the three highest peaks in Yorkshire – but seriously, how mountainous was Yorkshire, anyway? Kate filed this experience in her head as 'something to aim for next year' and resolved to start training in January.

Christmas itself passed fairly uneventfully in the end. The number of heads around the festive table was depleted by not one, but two, as Nick's elderly father had taken a turn for the worse and spent the day at home, mainly sleeping. A lump had lodged in Kate's throat all day, resolutely refusing to move, which made it difficult to eat with her usual gusto. And as they raised a toast to absent friends, a solitary tear escaped and rolled down Kate's cheek. However, when reflecting back on that first Christmas she concluded that there had been no drama, no tantrums and no 'I can't do this' moments; sadly, this was because there had been just a numbness, a nothingness, a gaping hole.

With January came a training schedule, of sorts. It wasn't that different to Kate's preparations for the Shine walk: they never made it further than fifteen miles during the five months leading up to the Three Peaks Challenge, which was a whopping eleven miles short of their target distance. Very often Kate and Emily both jumped at the chance to meet family or friends at the pub during one of their walks, which inevitably cut the whole thing short.

'Skiing would help us train,' claimed Emily during one of the walks, trying to sell the concept to Kate.

'Yeah, why not?' replied Kate. Her default position had become 'yes' to everyone and everything, for fear of being left behind alone and sad if she said 'no'.

In fact, their training schedule was enhanced, or rather interrupted, by not one but two holidays. Skiing in Val Thorens had quite literally got off to a rocky start when a landslide had caused a huge boulder to close the road leading to their destination. So the holiday had started in the wrong resort, which unsettled Kate more than she cared to admit. Feeling particularly fragile on this trip,

Kate missed Nick desperately throughout the whole holiday. She realised how much skiing had been 'their thing'.

Later on that spring, the whole family booked a trip to Cyprus. It was thought that some spring sun might help with healing. They had all suffered the after-effects of the shock of losing Nick, and they had all worked tirelessly to support Kate over the months, too. Unfortunately Kate was still suffering from what she termed the 'being in limbo' effect. The period between six and eighteen months after Nick's death was somehow the hardest: the raw shock had now worn off and with it had gone some of the protective layering that had cocooned itself around Kate. Other people had, naturally, moved on with their lives and at six months she found herself wondering what came next. Of course, the answer was 'nothing much', which then gave way to the feeling of being in limbo. It was far too soon to 'move on', yet enough time had passed that some sort of 'normality' was expected of her and by her. Kate felt trapped in her own existence and frequently questioned how she could take charge of things and change the course of her life in some way. Soon after Nick had died, Kate had had a chance encounter with a support worker from the local hospice. He was a retired financial advisor and the support he gave was to offer grieving relatives help on financial planning and the practical steps they could take to ease any money-related worries. He had been impressed by the level of Kate's financial organisation and had remarked that he could really do with someone like her to help him support others through his work in the hospice. She often reflected on that conversation and resolved many times to act on it during her 'limbo' period. But in truth she was scared to take a step back from full-time work in order to devote time to this cause, and her lack of gumption in the matter frustrated her.

After returning from their holiday in Cyprus, Kate and Emily had only six weeks before the Three Peaks Challenge. This was really the first time Kate had given the challenge more than a cursory thought, and it was at this point that Kate received an email asking her to sign a disclaimer for the event. As the world seemed to have become so litigious this did not disturb Kate unduly, but she promptly forgot all about it. Then one day in the middle of May she received another email asking for the signed form to be returned – urgently. Kate scanned through the form, finding herself reading parts of it aloud. 'Risks associated with the challenge… Your own responsibility… Blah, blah, blah… Wait – *what?*' Kate had got to the section that detailed the equipment needed; within the long list, hiking boots were identified as essential. Not desirable, or even recommended, but *essential*. 'Without them you will be refused entry,' the form stated. 'What the hell?' exclaimed Kate. All of her and Emily's training to date had been in trainers. There had been no thought or mention of hiking boots previously. Of course, as they later realised, if they had merely bothered to look at the website then the need for boots would have been completely obvious.

There was a flurry of activity that weekend to buy boots and break them in during the remaining ten days available. Who knew what a minefield buying hiking boots could be? Especially for two hapless sisters who were generally more interested in whether footwear went with the colour scheme of their outfits than the practicalities of ensuring their safe return from climbing three mountains. Decisions they had to make included lightweight versus heavy-duty, long versus short, winter versus summer. Once these aspects were narrowed down they had to choose colour, material, brand… The selection process went on all weekend and they even used what Kate described as 'a fake climbing ramp-type-thing' in one of the shops, to test-walk some of the pairs of boots. This ended in near-disaster when Kate caught her foot in a gap between the ramp and the wall, which propelled her forward into Emily, with the two of them collapsing into a heap. Kate tried to 'style it out' by announcing loudly: 'These boots are rubbish – I won't be buying them.' But she knew no one was falling for it.

In the end neither Kate nor Emily wore their boots more than twice before the big day, walking only a very short distance on each occasion. It was certainly not textbook preparation.

Letter to Nick.

Your Dad says that you all walked the Yorkshire Three Peaks back in the day when you and your brother were children. I wish I had listened more attentively when you talked about all of the hiking you did in your early years – I might just have learned something. He waxed lyrical about the exhilaration of the walk and the beauty of the landscape and he should know, being the artist in the family. He showed me some of the landscapes he had painted during one of his many visits to the area but said he only ever took on those mountain-climbs once. He says he's very proud of me taking on the challenge as it's tough.

Well, if he, your Mum and a couple of kids could do it back in the 1970s then so can I!

Widow, 42
seeks some sort of miracle to get her across twenty-six miles of gruelling Yorkshire terrain.

Chapter 15

With equal anxiousness Kate acknowledged the approach of the Three Peaks Challenge and the first anniversary of Nick's death. Perhaps this was why she had agreed so readily to take on Yorkshire; no amount of mulled wine or beer pong could have prevented her from noticing that the challenge date was a mere two days before the dreaded milestone. 'Something that stretches me and quite possibly causes me physical and mental anguish – that should be perfect for the occasion,' she had thought at one stage. 'Something so distracting that I simply can't think about the date… What's in a bloody date, anyway?' Kate had fought hard over that year to avoid being the person who constantly looked for reminders of what was lost in 'the first time doing this alone' and 'the first time experiencing that alone'. However, even she had to admit that the first anniversary of that tragic day was going to be a trial.

Just to add to the 'firsts' which pity-party Kate was experiencing, she also had her own birthday to contend with. Previously so happy to celebrate with friends and family, this year all she could do was 'get through it', as the day brought only debilitating sadness to her. She remembered with vivid clarity her birthday two years earlier, when they had received the gut-wrenching confirmation of Nick's terminal illness. Walking away from the consultant, the nurse and even poor Nick himself, Kate had locked herself in the disabled toilet at the run-down hospital, before sinking to her knees in despair. She remembered the hours and hours of silence between her and Nick, both desperately trying to understand what they had been told, and failing. She remembered the realisation that her life had just changed for ever.

The build-up to the Three Peaks Challenge had therefore been less than smooth. Work had been particularly busy during the preceding week, so as a consequence Kate was more stressed and less rested than she would have liked. However, it was an adventure – as she and Emily jumped into the car for the journey north, there was an excitement between them with the knowledge that they were heading towards the complete unknown. Neither of them had ever taken on anything quite so challenging before.

Despite leaving at lunchtime, they found the Friday traffic especially bad. The M25 was its normal charmless self, but beyond that every single road they took seemed to mock their attempts to head north – almost as if saying to them, 'Why bother?' Seven hours after they had started their journey, both the weary travellers were indeed wondering why they had bothered. But just at that moment they took in their surroundings. Barely ten minutes from the B&B they had booked, the countryside suddenly opened out into the most stunning vista. Rolling hills lined with dry-stone walls, vast trees of the deepest of deep greens and—

'Oh my Jesus Christ!' exclaimed Kate. 'Em, is *that* what we're climbing tomorrow?'

Ahead of them was the biggest hill that Kate had seen, in England at least, and certainly the biggest one that she would ever, in a million years, have considered climbing. Her sister shrieked. They both looked at each other and dissolved into nervous fits of laughter. 'No backing out now,' said Emily. 'That's probably not even one of the peaks we're doing.' It turned out later that she was right – the mountains they had to climb were much worse!

They arrived in time to meet some of the others in the group they would be walking with. Eating sensibly and staying away from the bar was the plan for the evening. The B&B they were staying in was a very pretty stone building of traditional construction. It exuded charm from first impressions, with pretty pink wild roses growing all around the entrance and lovingly tended gardens. There were squeals of delight and excitement as Kate and Emily joined the small party of walkers, including the lovely Rachel, in the bar. They quickly settled down to eat some much-needed food, in a very rudimentary attempt to provide enough fuel for the challenge of the following day. This aspect of walking was something that Kate struggled with immensely. She found that she experienced real highs and lows of energy throughout lengthy hikes, and recalled this being a real issue on that first charity walk in London. She remembered how the three of them had set out full of chatter and nervous energy, but had quickly subsided into a mid-walk lull which had lasted at least five miles. Luckily the array of sugary sweets they had brought did a certain something to lift Kate's energy. This time, however, she knew that she would need to be a little more scientific in her approach, with double the distance of Shine and three peaks to cover during at least a twelve-hour period of non-stop walking.

Kate being Kate though, this 'scientific' approach stretched no further than a nod to needing some slow-burn energy from carbs. The extent of her knowledge took her to that point, but she didn't go beyond what she already knew. This aspect of her own behaviour annoyed her – and she was sure it must annoy others around her, too. She had been naturally quite inquisitive up until recent times, but then it had been as though she had hit forty-something and subconsciously said: 'Right, that's it – I know everything I know now, so that will just have to get me by.' For a while she had blamed this attitude on the grief of losing Nick, having no room for inquiry because that would mean opening up her mind, which felt like a dangerous thing to do. However, this seemed to have become a habit and she felt strongly that she ought to change it.

For some reason Kate had even chosen to ignore the fact that her dearest – 'oldest living' – friend Katherine had a sports physiology degree and therefore could have written her a whole nutrition plan for the occasion! But in the absence of a plan or much knowledge, the extent of Kate's preparation ran to eating some spaghetti

Bolognese that night. However, she was in the company of friends and in a beautiful part of the world, so mentally she was now in a great place, and looking forward to the challenge ahead.

The friends, old and new, were chatting and discussing how long it might take them to finish the hike (while Kate was secretly wondering whether she would finish at all) when one asked, 'What have you brought for your packed lunch tomorrow?' A bolt of electricity immediately went through Kate as she and Emily looked at each other, knowing neither one had even considered lunch for the following day.

'Errrm...' Kate's reply started.

Rachel jumped in. 'Oh dear,' she said. 'I didn't think of that either!'

She had, at least partially, saved Kate's blushes in front of this new group of hiking friends. Rachel had been a stalwart friend to Kate over the preceding twelve months. They had worked together for a number of years – but then their work friendship had morphed into a real kinship during the period of Nick's illness. Rachel's idea to take on the Yorkshire Three Peaks Challenge had ignited a possibly life-long interest for Kate in hiking, for which she would be eternally grateful to this kindest of friends.

'We could ask the kitchen if they will make us something,' suggested Rachel, ever the practical solution-giver in all situations.

'Great idea!' replied Kate, heading off in the direction of the bar.

During their conversation with the kitchen staff at the bar, the hapless travellers realised they had also not thought about the fact that they would need earlier-than-possible breakfast the next morning. Luckily the B&B was situated so close to the start point for the Three Peaks Challenge that they were well-versed in providing a light and appropriate packed breakfast for the morning of the hike. So with both meals arranged, Kate, Emily and Rachel could go back to enjoying what was left of their evening. They made the most of the time in finalising plans for their forthcoming trip to Glastonbury Festival – which had been another one of Kate's 'yeah, let's just do it' moments.

The morning of the hike was 'early, too bloody early', according to Emily, who really wasn't the best of morning people. The make-in-the-pot porridge that they had been given did not hit the spot, being too watery and too stodgy all at the same time, which was a feat in itself. They made a cup of tea, but that didn't really work, either. So the twenty-six miles that lay ahead would be attempted with little more than half a pot of porridge and an apple between them. Kate didn't stop to worry about this – what was the use? They had brought plenty of energy bars, some water and energy gel, which was a whole new concept to the two sisters. Neither had tried it before, but the idea of an immediate energy boost when required seemed a useful one, so it had gone into the rucksack. There had been much debate about how many of the energy bars they should pack, and which flavours. The whole experience was so new to Kate and Emily that they had no concept of what they would need or even want during the day ahead.

Walking out into the chilly May morning, Kate noted the residue of the preceding week's torrential rain. As she picked her way round the many puddles in the car park she noticed they were being slowly lit by the sunrise, looming over the vast, lush landscape that domineered all around them. She had settled on packing merely her food and water supplies into her small rucksack, eschewing her waterproof trousers and keeping her fingers crossed for a dry day. The rucksack was not only small but also woefully unsuitable. It was in fact a freebie she had kept from a fun rugby trip to France several years previously, which meant it had none of the qualities that hikers look for: it was not waterproof, it was not big enough, it was not padded, and it was not capable of storing water 'on tap' – something which Kate noticed was the way of things amongst keen hiking-types.

There were promises of much more rain to come that weekend.

Kate looked up at the sky. 'Please keep off until tomorrow,' she begged.

<u>Letter to Nick.</u>

I need you by my side today. Better still, behind me kicking my butt all the way. In death you are still my inspiration, as you were in life. Em has decided upon a strategy of 2 ibuprofen every 4 hours, regardless of pain or fatigue levels. I may well do the same.

Widow, 43
seeks a proper packed lunch, or she will never make it to the finish line within the allotted twelve hours.

Chapter 16

The short drive to the starting point was unusually quiet: Kate and Rachel were deep in thought about what to expect, while Emily was never communicative in the mornings anyway. The quaintly-named Horton-in-Ribblesdale was their destination, a short distance away. As they arrived Kate was struck by just how many people were already piling into this small village, tucked in amongst the Yorkshire Dales, and she now realised the scale of the event she had signed up to. Even though there were only fifteen or so people in the group she was walking with, there must have been at least ten other groups of a similar size already in the area. All around her walkers were chatting, lacing up sturdy-looking boots and loading rucksacks onto shoulders.

'Wait a minute, they've all got walking poles!' Kate exclaimed. It turned out that although not an obligatory part of the kit for the event, the vast majority of participants had opted for poles. Kate and Emily were left feeling slightly amateurish and vulnerable.

After Kate had visited the public toilet in the car park no fewer than three times in ten minutes, her group walked round to the Life-Changing Challenges area, which was clearly marked in an adjacent field by tall flag-banners, furiously flapping in the wind. It turned out that the group had hired the services of a company which provided guides for the day – experts not only in hiking, but also in motivating people for this sort of situation. The group gathered for a quick pre-start selfie, which made Kate laugh when she thought about it later. There she was in a strange combination of hiking boots and jogging bottoms (not very technical ones), several layers comprising T-shirt, fleece and rain mac (again, not technical, just a run-of-the-mill spotty blue one she had bought at a market) – all topped off with a woolly hat and sunglasses. The hat had become her new prized possession. It was from her old polo club: there on the front of the dark blue beanie rose the mighty white horse of the club's logo… riding a bike, of course! For Kate was no high-goal, high-brow horse polo player – she was a 'retired' bike polo player, who had been increasingly thinking about the camaraderie of those polo days and wondering whether she should seek to go back.

Kate and Emily were introduced to the rest of the walking group, who were mainly people Rachel knew from her new role at work. There was a tall and classically handsome man of Nordic descent. His name was, of course, Jurgen and he was blond and athletic. 'You couldn't make this up,' thought Kate. However, she found him a little aloof. She guessed that one look at her made him realise that he wouldn't be spending much time with her on the hike – 'on account of finishing about three hours before me,' thought Kate, as she smiled and greeted him. Jurgen's girlfriend Astrid was friendly, though, and chatted animatedly about her life since recently moving to Leeds, and the weather. It amused Kate to think that she had been indoctrinated into English small-talk so quickly.

The main organiser of the party was a friendly Yorkshireman called David, who was in his sixties. Rachel didn't seem to rate him as a boss, but he seemed pleasant enough. He was very tall but was walking with a pronounced limp which, Rachel explained, was due to on-going recovery from a badly shattered leg.

'Apparently he's been told he shouldn't really be doing this so early on in the recovery process,' Rachel informed her friends. 'But being the organiser, he felt he couldn't drop out.' Secretly Kate was pleased: this meant there was surely one person who might be as slow as her, and who might not even finish?

Life-Changing Challenges had provided three expert guides for the day, who gave everyone a safety talk, covering such important topics as 'don't wander off the path into bogs' and 'don't throw yourself off mountain paths'. Dressed in smart black walking-trousers and technical jackets with the company's orange logo emblazoned on them, the expert guides all had walking poles too, which Kate thought could be useful in a sticky situation at least. They finished preparations, gathered the expectant group together and finally, after all of the anticipation, they were walking, heading towards the first of peaks.

At this stage they were one big chattering mass, all buoyed-up and ready for action. Kate looked around her, at people of all different shapes and sizes, all different ages and, of more interest to her, all different motivations for being there that day. She was always interested in people's back-stories, which she often simply made up in the absence of any factual evidence. A messy divorce here, a recovery from illness there: she often viewed things as though she were watching a movie. Sometimes, especially when life got particularly rough, she would even wonder if she was in her version of *The Truman Show*, thinking, 'Surely this must be some kind of test for me?' She expected that at some stage the director's voice would ring out through a hidden loudspeaker: 'Cut! That's enough – we don't need to put her through any more.' Somehow, this never happened, but it was comforting to think that one day it just might.

While Kate was busy chatting and wondering about people's back-stories, the first of the three peaks sneaked up on her and suddenly there it was: the craggy, rocky, slightly austere-looking Pen-y-ghent, daring her to take on this first challenge. It didn't rise up and loom over the walkers in the way that Kate had expected. Instead it just seemed to silently intimidate them with its hard-faced stoniness. Kate now realised why the organisers had absolutely insisted on the wearing of sturdy walking boots. The fell was almost exclusively made up of sizeable boulders, rocks, stones and was all-round rough terrain the whole way to the top, as far as she could see. With a little inward fist-punch, Kate steeled herself for this ascent – her first real test.

Rachel's boss David was walking near Kate at this point and started chatting about the times he had walked this peak in the past. He made the whole thing sound so everyday that Kate found the ascent much easier than anticipated. She even enjoyed the parts where walking became more of a scramble, using her hands and feet to navigate over the bigger rocks along the way. The mixed group soon started to spread out from one chatting cluster into sub-groups defined by youth, fitness, stature and outlook. 'What does it say about me,' wondered Kate, 'that I'm walking with a sixty-something-year-old who recently smashed his leg to bits and I'm barely keeping up with him?'

Emily and Rachel marched slightly ahead, which didn't surprise her: they both had youth and fitness on their side. Upon reaching the top Kate found Emily staging a 'jumping for joy' photo with the far-reaching landscape stretching out behind her. All Kate could manage was a slightly red-faced smile for her picture, while trying to remain standing atop the wind-blown summit – the first peak climbed with no help from a chair or drag-lift for both of the sisters. While Kate was busy regaining her breath, Rachel and Emily marched on. 'I see how this is going to be,' thought Kate, looking around her at the cluster of walkers who would probably remain her companions for the rest of the day, as she started to wend her way down the other side of Pen-y-ghent. She therefore experienced a small feeling of satisfaction when, several minutes later, she found Rachel somewhat 'stuck' by nerves. The going was even more rugged on the descent, making for challenging under-foot conditions, which clearly were not Rachel's strong point. Knowing that this would be the one time when she might actually manage to steal a march on Rachel, Kate picked her way – rather gracefully, she thought – down and past her friend with a small glow of happiness. 'Drink it up, Kate!' she said to herself. 'It's the only time you'll be ahead.'

Letter to Nick.

It was unfortunate that there were no pee-stops just when we needed them. I am pretty sure I heard your unmistakable laugh when I found what I thought was the perfect boulder to pee behind, only to turn around while pulling my trousers up to see a farmhouse overlooking said boulder. I didn't wait around to see if anyone was looking out!

Widow, 43
seeks a way to connect with new friends and has moved into the twenty-first century at last... She has a Facebook account!

Chapter 17

As the miles clocked up Kate realised that one of the real challenges of the day would be the lack of adrenaline on the long, flat walking sections which spanned out between each peak. While the fells demanded real physical effort, provoking the mental stimulation to keep going, the endless miles of flatness offered nothing more than a rest for the fiery throat and lungs from the previous exertion. After five or six miles the group paused for a drink, which was when the question of energy gel was raised.

'I hear that if your stomach is not used to it there can be unwelcome consequences,' announced Rachel, who was animatedly pointing towards her bum. This immediately put Kate off, needing no further detail.

Unwrapping an energy bar instead, Kate bit expectantly in and immediately regretted it. 'It's like chewing bloody cardboard!' she exclaimed. She knew she was overstating the truth a little, but nonetheless she had expressed her lack of satisfaction with the snack. Overstating the situation was something Kate excelled at: why just say she didn't like something, when instead she could liken it to the worst thing she had ever tasted? One of her favourite sayings to that end was to claim, 'The last time I tasted something like that I was trying to kill myself.' This was of course used for dramatic effect, having no basis in reality. Kate liked big, she liked bold, and she certainly felt that she ended up in plenty of dramas.

Throwing the energy bar back into her rucksack, Kate chose another – which left her equally unimpressed. 'Oh no... this *is* going to be a long day,' she thought.

Rachel, meanwhile, was on a mission to prove what she could do. She had taken the challenge far more seriously than Kate and as such was marching on ahead again. Rachel had worked hard to improve her fitness over the preceding months, so how could Kate begrudge her that small victory? 'We hate it when our friends become successful,' Kate thought secretly, channelling the Morrissey song. However, when the welcome lunch stop approached, Kate easily caught up with both Rachel and Emily, so the three of them enjoyed a short rest and a snack together. They marvelled at the magnificent viaduct ahead of them: twenty-four huge red-brick arches spanning Ribble Valley, at what Kate reasoned must be over 100 feet at the viaduct's highest point. The beauty of the Yorkshire Dales combined with this masterpiece of Victorian engineering would normally have called for a slow and quite possibly boozy lunch for Kate – but this rest stop was restricted to ten minutes and half a sandwich (they all feared that more than this would result in exercise-induced vomit).

As the whole walking group started out again there was a rekindled air of anticipation as they knew the next big challenge lay ahead, in the form of the second peak. It had been clearly visible during their lunch stop, but it wasn't until they started the ascent about three or four miles further on that Kate realised that Whernside completely dwarfed anything that had gone before. 'It makes the viaduct look like a small child's toy,' she thought. 'It rises out of the earth like a—'

'Shit!' she said out loud. 'It's a proper mountain!'

She realised she had just stated what was obvious to the whole group; Kate often felt she needed to verbalise her thoughts and today was certainly going to be no exception. Panic jolted through her as she remembered again that she really was walking twenty-six miles and she really was hiking up three mountains. Was she capable of completing the challenge?

Fairly soon into the ascent, the group became very strung-out again. This was mentally challenging for Kate, who usually thrived on joint experiences, gaining positive energy from those around her.

Equally, however, and nowadays more than ever, Kate would suffer badly if surrounded by negative energy. To this end she had learned to become quite insular when required, in order to focus on herself and achieve her chosen goal. Thirty minutes into the Whernside ascent, Kate made the mistake of looking far ahead to see that, despite having kept a decent pace throughout, she must only have climbed about an eighth of the way towards the summit. This was a blow to her confidence. She was just digging in and focusing on herself, looking for some inner strength, when she noticed one of the guides walking alongside her.

'Hey, how's it going?' he enquired cheerfully. Barely out of puff and built like a whippet, Nathan was a welcome diversion from the dark clouds that had started to circle Kate's head at this point. Dressed in black, he was equipped with all the latest technical clothing, a large rucksack and walking poles. In short, he looked the part – which was comforting to Kate, as she neither felt nor looked the part herself.

'Oh, well, you know,' she replied as cheerily as she could, before carrying on very honestly: 'If I had any means of escape right now, I would.'

Nathan laughed and continued the conversation. He had a natural ease and it seemed that he could talk as easily as he could hike, chatting about the beauty of the landscape, what Kate did for a living and, naturally, the weather. In fact, the chat was so easy-going that Kate felt the climb far less than she had up until then (which she realised was Nathan's tactic) and before she knew it, they were three-quarters of the way to the summit. She had discovered all about Nathan and his business of organising and guiding 'life-changing challenges' across the country – to the point that she had almost committed herself to an event local to her which they would be running later in the year. Nathan, in turn, had learned a fair amount about Kate: her likes and dislikes, her hobbies, her job. During the conversation they had also caught up with Emily. It seemed that the power of chat had increased Kate's speed – no surprise for someone whose school reports had invariably described her as 'chatty', 'lively' or simply 'easily distracted'. So this was the key: someone just needed to carry on distracting her for the next six or seven hours, and all would be well.

'So, this must be Merlot?' asked Nathan.

'Huh?' was Kate's bemused reply.

'I have you down as Shiraz,' he explained, 'so it stands to reason your sister would be Merlot.' Clearly he really *had* been listening as Kate had talked her way up the never-ending ascent!

When the two sisters and their able and affable guide reached the summit of Whernside Kate's spirits were truly lifted. She had a fab new nickname, she was enjoying the challenge again, and conquering the second of three peaks that day was quite an achievement. They took a few minutes to look around them and drink in the pure mountain air. Far in the distance lay the Lake District and Morecambe Bay. The views from this highest point in Yorkshire were as breath-taking as the climb up had been. Staring towards Cumbria, Kate smiled as she thought of her good friend Candice, who lived there. The Lake District often seemed about as far away from Kate's corner of south-east England as one could get; so standing there, staring across the hills and mountains, Kate reached out with her eyes and her heart and sent a little message of love to her beautiful friend, hoping she would feel it that day.

'Did you know the fastest finisher of this challenge was two hours and forty-six minutes?' Nathan's voice broke through the moment. 'Girls, come on, let's get going!'

Over the ensuing few miles the sheer relief of having only one peak to go naturally boosted Kate, so she didn't even mind the fact that Rachel and Emily were striding on ahead again. By now she was settled with a fairly regular sub-group of four walking companions, including Nathan, who had clearly either fallen on his sword or drawn the short straw of motivating the slower people at the back of the party. He continued to do a sterling job of keeping them occupied – even if he and Kate didn't always see eye-to-eye. Around the nineteen-mile point, Nathan was revelling in the beauty of the landscape and invited the small party to appreciate it too. All Kate could muster in response was a grunt and a mumble: 'I would if I even had the energy to raise my eyes.' This seemed to irritate Nathan a little.

'I've heard it all before,' was his parting shot as he walked ahead.

The final peak was dead ahead when the navigation towards it became much trickier. Rolling fields gave way to a scrubby landscape littered with boulders and huge, possibly purpose-laid, slabs of light-grey granite. The ground to either side of these slabs was boggy, which Kate found out by accident, making her very glad indeed of her waterproof walking boots. Three-quarters of the way through the hike and still those boots – and her feet – were holding up nicely. This felt like nothing short of a miracle, given that she had only worn them twice before the big day.

Letter to Nick.

It was lovely of your Dad to text me wishing me luck during this massive challenge. The exchange of texts provided a welcome distraction for a few minutes while we took a small break. I can hardly convey my shock and horror, though, at finding out that your family hadn't in fact completed this challenge quite so quickly all those years ago! The text exchange was priceless:

'Hi Kate, just wanted you to know I am proud and impressed with what you are doing this week, good luck throughout. Which peak are you climbing today?'

'Hi Tony, thanks, so thoughtful of you. A little confused with your question as I am climbing ALL 3 of the peaks today...'

'Oh gosh, that's amazing, I didn't realise it was even possible to complete all in one day!'

'But you did it back in the day Tony!'

'No, we did it over 4 days and that was hard enough.'

> **Widow, 43**
> seeks new inspiration
> to finish this walk.

Chapter 18

'I *can't*,' said Kate, very simply but with determination.

Standing at the foot of the final mountain they had to climb that day, she had decided that Ingleborough was a challenge too far. Exhausted from nearly ten hours of walking, Kate's legs were complaining, her lungs were combusting and her spirit was crushed. She gazed at dozens of walkers navigating their way up the most rugged of the peaks, scrambling along on all-fours for the most part. They disappeared up and up, becoming ants in the distance. Defiance gave way to some sneaky tears. Kate hated crying in public but could not hold the tears back at this stage. Then Nathan popped up with his insufferable fitness, almost jogging towards her and looking ready to bound up the 2,300-foot climb in a single leap.

'Come on – last big effort,' he said lightly. One look at Kate's face, streaked with tears, must have told him that he needed to change tack with her. Brandishing his walking pole at her, his voice changed to a shout: 'Get up that bloody hill or you'll get this up your arse!'

Nathan was clearly a great judge of character, as this indeed marked the turning-point for Kate. It was an approach she understood and his choice of language resonated with her. She sprang onto the first rock and didn't look back. As she scrambled her way up the first part of the ascent she actually found herself enjoying this new challenge. 'I'm doing *real* climbing,' she thought to herself with pride.

About halfway up, she had to navigate past several people who were sitting contemplating life, temporarily unable to summon up the mental metal required to continue. For Ingleborough was certainly the most challenging peak in terms of its rugged steepness, presenting a frightening prospect for the faint-of-heart or for anyone who dared to look down at any point. Kate kept her eyes firmly ahead and used anything to hand which she could hang on to. She didn't suffer any need to 'look good', so scrabbling and scrambling as she went, her last push was energetic and effective.

Lack of concern about how she looked to the outsider was something Kate was thankful for. It was less inhibiting in life, though at times her friends did not agree. On one occasion a few years before, Kate, Katherine and Candice had gone on a tree-top climbing adventure. Kate had not realised that somehow over the years she had developed a slight fear of heights – it was nothing debilitating in her everyday life, but it was enough to make her less than totally comfortable swinging around in trees, even with a harness. They had all navigated their way across a rickety rope bridge and had then completed a challenge which, to all intents and purposes, had felt like they were walking the plank. By then Kate had voiced her new-found dislike of heights and had been ably reassured by the others – before reaching her nemesis. Standing on the edge of a wooden platform, she was faced with a ten-foot rope-swing onto a cargo net. It could have been a hundred-foot gap as far as Kate was concerned, as she was going absolutely nowhere. She had planted her feet and resolutely refused to move, frozen to the spot. Katherine and Candice had called out words of encouragement, becoming more and more frantic as a big crowd started to gather, but still Kate had refused to move. It hadn't mattered who was watching. Katherine had counted her down from ten, in an attempt to get things moving. It had been a great idea, but Kate had simply shouted, 'You can count as much as you like, but I'm not bloody moving!'

Eventually Kate had taken that swing. Candice later liked to joke that people from surrounding towns and villages heard Kate's screams as she went, and that children had to be ushered away from her strong and creative language. When Kate had hit the cargo net, she had grabbed hold of it so tightly that two days afterwards she could still see the rope imprint on her fingers. There she had stayed for at least twenty minutes until she had mustered up the courage to climb down to safety. That had marked the end of Kate's tree-top adventures.

Now here she was, at the top of the final Yorkshire peak and feeling energised by a great sense of achievement. Rachel and Emily were ahead, but all was well with the world: she had faced down that brief moment of total resignation at the bottom of the fell and was now back in charge, thanks to threats of violence from a guide and his walking pole.

'Good job!' rang out Nathan's voice from a few feet in front. 'So... Just around this corner is the ascent to the real summit.'

Kate's stomach lurched.

'*What?*' Her heart thumped and she experienced a rush of blood to the head. 'Are you actually joking?' she enquired, slightly angrily.

It turned out that Nathan was absolutely not joking: Ingleborough had a 'false peak'. Common opinion was that you needed to walk another ten minutes beyond this 'summit' to get to the real summit.

'I'm not bothered about getting to that pointy bit,' Kate claimed. But she was persuaded by the other members of the group that their impressive achievements so far would be slightly marred if they didn't actually reach the top of this last mountain. So off they trudged, Kate less in charge than she had felt two minutes earlier.

The real summit was eerie. Kate likened it to a sort of moonscape: rocky and barren, everything grey. Despite the fact that there were several fellow hikers making the journey, there was a quiet air of mystery about it.

'So this is it,' thought Kate as she looked around her. 'I've done it.'

She didn't realise that the hardest part of the challenge was yet to come.

While climbing to the real summit Kate had passed Rachel and Emily on their way back down. They had told Kate that they were trying for the sub-twelve-hour target for the day, so would be jogging on ahead.

'I see – every man for himself, is it?' was all Kate had summoned up in reply, even though deep down she understood and was quite comfortable with this plan. With approximately five miles to go, the twelve-hour deadline didn't seem totally unreasonable for her sister and Rachel to achieve. Kate had always harboured lower expectations for herself, on the basis that she would be delighted to merely finish and still be alive. By now she was walking with a select sub-group of the broken and the unfit, with Nathan still by their side motivating, cajoling and entertaining. It was incredible how hard those last five miles were. All on the flat or downhill, the distance stretched out ahead of them seemingly for ever. By now fatigued and undernourished (not at all a normal occurrence for Kate), it felt like they had exhausted all topics of conversation and had to dig deep in silence.

At that point Nathan asked Kate why she had chosen the Three Peaks Challenge.

'Oh, you know, a drunken plan at a Christmas party,' was her initial reply. This was based on truth, of course, but it did not convey one of the reasons why Kate had started choosing challenges in general. 'Truth be told,' she went on, 'I just want to feel alive again since I lost my husband.' That still sounded odd to Kate as she heard herself say it. Would she ever get used to using this language and carrying the label of 'widow'?

'Here – have a jelly baby,' came Nathan's reply. This was good for both of them, stopping Kate from complete disclosure.

Unlike the conclusion of Shine London, in Yorkshire Kate found no cheering crowds, no finish line as such and therefore no triumphant end to the day. Yet the sense of achievement and pure relief she felt, as she glimpsed the little village she had left nearly thirteen hours ago, was immense. The last of the group to limp home consisted of Kate, Rachel's boss with the smashed leg, and Jurgen's girlfriend Astrid, who had been a very acceptable companion for those last five miles. Nathan had abandoned them towards the end, figuring that even Kate, David and Astrid could manage to make it from a mile out without getting lost or broken.

As she crossed the railway track into Horton, Kate looked around her. Where were Emily, Rachel and the rest of the gang? She ferreted around in her rucksack for her phone and called them. No reply from Emily. No reply from Rachel. No reply from Emily again. Kate decided to walk to the car, thinking that if she stopped anywhere now she might never make it there. The relief as she took her walking boots off was instant – her feet didn't know whether to thank her or throttle her in that moment.

'Em?' Kate answered her phone when it rang ten minutes later. Her sister sounded way jollier than she ought to.

'We're in the pub down the road,' explained Emily. 'Onto our second pint. Want a drink?'

On reflection, Kate decided she did – but had no intention of walking to meet them. So she and Astrid drove the hundred metres to the Crown and joined the others. There was much patting of backs and sharing of stories, before they decided that food was the next priority. As night drew in they collected their 'completers' T-shirts and headed back to their B&B, for some more liquid refreshment with a bit of dinner on the side.

Letter to Nick.

I met a guide today who helped me achieve something I really wasn't sure I could. He motivated, cajoled, inspired and bullied me up those mountains and then chatted and allowed me to chat all the way back down the other side each time. Did he sense there was something more to my challenge today, something that drove me on regardless of the fatigue and exhaustion? Did he really want me to share my story? I guess by the fact that he sidled off as I was talking that he was simply chatting and hadn't expected to be stand-in counsellor in the absence of Audrey – there I went, oversharing as normal!

Widow, 43
seeks new challenge.

Chapter 19

Having come away from the epic Yorkshire walk virtually unscathed, Kate felt that she was on a roll and was looking forward to her next adventure. She had known that the day after returning from the Three Peaks Challenge weekend the calendar would tip her into that dreaded moment: a year since Nick had died. What was she expecting? A lightning strike? An earthquake? She wasn't sure, but instead what she had was a fairly normal day, with no dramas and, in the end, no tears. For that was the thing Kate had come to notice the most over the preceding twelve months – that the 'big occasions' rarely caused big reactions, whereas tears always came at the least expected, and often most unwanted, moments. She remembered an incident the month before when she had tried to sneakily park in a loading bay to pop into a shop. A delivery driver had, quite reasonably and politely, asked if she could move up so he could unload. She had dissolved into floods of tears and driven off like a madwoman, leaving the poor man standing there totally bemused. Kate had long ago given up trying to understand what would set her off like this and instead just chose to roll with it. She did wonder whether widows should be issued with badges, like the ones expectant mothers wear on London transport. Instead of 'Baby on board' it could say 'Beware, no control of emotions', or 'Spinster-in-waiting'. As she often asked herself: 'When will I stop being the "poor widow" and become a bloody spinster?'

Her next adventure was, in fact, just a few days away and as the pilgrimage to Glastonbury drew nearer, so did the realisation that soon she would be peeing in all sorts of unsanitary places in the heart of Somerset. Kate had eagerly agreed to be part of the hopeful ticket-buying syndicate which had formed back in October the previous year. At that point she was still grabbing all opportunities to say yes and be involved, no matter what the occasion. Getting tickets for Glastonbury was the mortal version of Jason's quest for the Golden Fleece, so Kate had happily joined a group who all committed to pool the tickets if they managed to buy any.

With her sister at the helm there had been a military precision to the whole process, with six of them having agreed to be ready and waiting with various mobile devices primed for the airwaves to open. On the morning when the tickets went on sale, Kate had had her usual techno-meltdown. None of her devices had worked, which she recognised was probably more to do with user error than interference from some kind of black hole. Still, there had always been some kind of kinetic forcefield surrounding Kate. All sorts of incidents with electronic equipment seemed to happen around her, and not just because she was the clumsiest bull-in-a-china-shop of all time. Nick used to call her 'Carrie', from the Stephen King novel, and she rarely put up much defence against this. She had to admit that when she was in a room odd things happened to innocent pieces of hardware that just lay around minding their own business. She had once recounted her nickname to a colleague at work and then during a road trip with the very same colleague his mobile phone and iPad had stopped working – at which point she had been banned from car-sharing for ever. Nevertheless, despite Kate's lack of input for Glastonbury, one of the hopeful six had managed to secure tickets to the Mecca of music festivals – so now they were ready, hot on the heels of Yorkshire's life-changing challenge and careering towards five days of pure hedonism in the mud.

Luckily for Kate, who was clueless about such matters, when it came to festivals there was no more seasoned a professional than Emily. She had the whole operation down to such a fine art that Kate felt sure even Michael Eavis himself might do well to consult her on a thing or two. There was an unspoken agreement that neither of the sisters would be camping. Kate had tried it once when she was seventeen and had resolutely announced that she would never ever be doing it again, especially not beyond the age of forty. If asked to name just a few of the drawbacks, from her point of view, she would cite the obvious ones: lack of privacy, shared facilities, lack of space. But also there were the seasonal variables: too cold, too wet, too hot. All of this without even mentioning lack of electricity, lack of running water, no mirrors, no hanging-space and, in her opinion, the general nastiness of it all. So the group had collectively agreed to hire two motor-homes, which pretty much eliminated all the aforementioned problems and offered them the possibility of a Glastonbury to remember. When it came down to it, though, things weren't that easy, because it seemed that every single person in the UK had had the same idea for that weekend in June. The only vehicles available were dotted around the four corners of the country. Luckily, Emily was always happy to be side-tracked from work and had thrown herself into arrangements for finding suitable motor-homes. Never mind that they were located over 200 miles from home; she and three friends were more than happy to extend the road trip and collect the vehicles, leaving Kate and Rachel to make their own way down to Glastonbury the following day.

Finally, months of planning and preparation were over and Kate found herself on the train heading towards Heathrow, where she would meet Rachel. Somehow Rachel had devised a convoluted way of getting to Glastonbury via Israel, of all places, as her exciting new job had made her an overnight globetrotter, no less. 'The girl from Yorkshire done good!' thought Kate.

The planning and preparation had in reality been Emily's: all Kate had done was follow Emily's instructions, not very well, and stuffed some random clothes in a bag. In fact, it was not until Kate was leaving her front door that she remembered the need for bedding, hurriedly pushing some old pillows and a duvet into a black sack as she ran back through the house. Waiting for Rachel at the airport, bags in hand, she felt nervous with anticipation and excitement – so much so, that when Rachel walked out of Arrivals towards her, they both squealed with delight and ran to greet each other, hugging and jumping all at the same time. There was the mundane task of picking up Rachel's car from Long Stay Parking, but then their adventure began.

Dusk gave way to night during the journey west, but it was very nearly the longest day of the year, so a gradual fading of the light revealed the most sumptuous velvety night sky accompanied by a bright crystal moon. When they were near Pilton it became lighter, as the rose-gold glow from the mighty festival site rose above the 900-acre farm, almost as if the sun were rising from within it. Despite the deeply rural location, all roads led to Glastonbury Festival and Kate couldn't help but feel sorry for the local residents of the area, whose lives must be fairly intolerable for several weeks before, during and after the event. People who had chosen a quiet, rural lifestyle over the buzz and hubbub of town or city life were subjected to the transit of hundreds of thousands of extra people descending on their little corner of the world each year, without so much as a 'thank you' as they passed through. These strangers came from all corners of the globe, travelling by planes, trains and automobiles, not to mention bikes, helicopters and convoys of vans and lorries that must have played their part in building the infrastructure of the festival for weeks on end.

Kate considered herself relatively well travelled and felt she had sampled many outstanding experiences throughout her life. However, nothing could have prepared her for the sight of Glastonbury Festival when she first saw it on the approach.

Wending their way through the narrow country lanes, the two travellers found that they were actually up above the site, looking down on it from the car. As they approached, they both gasped at the scale of what seemed to be the most enormous fun fair in the world.

'And most people haven't even arrived yet,' said Rachel. 'Imagine what it will be like from tomorrow!'

Certainly, the consolation of arriving in the dead of night was that they avoided the scrum that would start the following day. Since Glastonbury seemed to have a twenty-four-hour culture, their arrival time only had a bearing on whether they would find a bed for the night. In the worst case, failure to locate Emily and the others would result in Kate and Rachel sleeping in the car – which they had already decided wouldn't be too bad.

Rachel's swanky new red Mercedes glided along the lanes with ease. 'I wonder how easily it will glide out of the parking field if it rains,' thought Kate secretly. Rain being an intrinsic part of festival lore, it seemed likely that this year would be no exception. However, on the night they arrived, all the signs seemed to indicate that rain would stay away. The forecast was positive, the sky was clear and Kate would describe it as 'set fair', to recall a well-used term from her Grandad Leslie's day.

Grandad Leslie: just the thought of him would always bring a smile to Kate's face. The thought evoked the moving line of poetry which seemed to explain so well how she felt about special people in her life, just as Elizabeth Barrett Browning had felt about her lover when she wrote it: 'How do I love thee? Let me count the ways.'

Even years after his death, little 'Leslieisms' would frequently pop into Kate's head and make her spontaneously laugh out loud. He had created and maintained an 'edgy grandad' persona – none of your little old greying man with a walking stick. None of your 'there, there, there' sympathetic ear for wounded soldiers and broken hearts. Leslie had been all about living in the moment, seizing opportunities and, quite frankly, manning up to life's undulations. This hadn't surprised anyone, given that his father (who Leslie would describe as a 'man of the cross') had died when Leslie was a small boy, leaving all his money to the Church, and none to his now-penniless family. Hence the oft-used phrase in Leslie's repertoire, 'the nearer the cross, the bigger the hypocrite'.

Kate credited Grandad Leslie for her strength of character and sense of humour, in addition to her sense of justice and fairness in everything. She also credited him for furnishing her with the most extensive range of colourful language a girl could possess! He would invoke such language when reprimanding dogs, cats and children alike, but it was especially effective when targeting annoying intruders into his busy life. There was the infamous letter he had written to the bank, for instance, who had made some mistake with his financial matters, causing him unnecessary stress and inconvenience; it started with 'Dear Pig-Fuckers'. Kate knew that Grandad Leslie had not been an unjust man, but he had not suffered fools gladly, especially if they had wasted his time.

Such was the size of the festival that it was a full twenty minutes after they had first seen the site when Rachel's car pulled into the entrance. Darkness had fully enveloped the rest of the country, but this little corner of the world was alight and buzzing with life. Emily had advised them to try to drive straight over to the motor-home parking area, so they could unload the Mercedes before taking it to where all the car parks were, seemingly a million miles away. Steeled for a fight with fluorescent-tabard-wearing parking attendants, both travellers were almost disappointed at how easy it was for them to gain access to the motor-home parking area. Sure enough, as Emily had described, their two motor-homes took pride of place directly opposite the entrance to the festival site, resplendent with striped awnings, tables and chairs laid out between the two vehicles – and seemingly deserted. The evidence showed that before heading off in search of festival fun, Emily and her companions had enjoyed some lively entertainment already. A discarded beer pong table looked forlorn, strewn with plastic pint glasses. A solitary ping-pong ball lay in the grass.

Letter to Nick.

Music and beer - the perfect combo as far as you would have been concerned. Would we ever have given ourselves the chance to do this if you were still around? Perhaps by the time we were eighty years old we would have had enough money! Yet another thing to be thankful for - I am spending your money with guilt and pleasure all at once. You're missing out on beer pong festival fun and I know you would bloody love this one!

Widow, 43
seeks sister, who is somewhere in this 900-acre site!

Chapter 20

'Where are you?' Kate shouted down the phone.

By now it was well past midnight and they were trying to locate Emily so that they could get hold of the all-important festival passes and gain access to their motor-home. Kate and Rachel could hardly complain, because they were the latecomers. Emily and her three friends had driven the 200-odd miles to Devon to collect both motor-homes, before immediately driving a further two hours in a different direction again to get them to Glastonbury. By leaving ridiculously early they had been the first people to arrive at the motor-home parking area, and had therefore bagged the mother of all parking spots. Emily and her friends had booked, planned, collected and delivered Kate and Rachel's luxury accommodation, so that the two festival-virgins could simply arrive and ease themselves into Glastonbury life.

'I'm on my way,' came Emily's breathless and slightly slurred reply. 'I may have had a couple of drinks,' she giggled. 'I'll be about twenty minutes.'

Mornings in Glastonbury, it turned out some hours later, were slow-moving and eerily quiet – who knew that after a heavy night of partying, festival-goers would want a lie-in? Contrary to Kate's normal up-with-the-larks approach at home, she knew she needed to relax into this alternative way of life and adopt it as her own for the next few days. Lazing around in bed in her luxury motor-home, she was pondering what the day would hold, when she heard a rapping on the door. Assuming it was Emily, Kate jumped out of bed in her knickers and, donning a huge blue 'monster' hat en route, flung the door open. Looking back at Kate was a fairly dazed parking attendant who managed to say, 'You need to move the Mercedes to the public car park,' before scuttling off.

Rachel laughed from her bunk over the cab of the vehicle. 'He must see all sorts over the weekend, though,' she said, trying to console Kate.

Car parked, motor-home organised, and rucksacks packed with the bare essentials (booze and hand sanitiser), the group were finally ready to explore the site. Resplendent with their Glastonbury guides hanging like medallions from their necks, and with their prized wristbands firmly in place, they entered the hallowed ground. Miles of marquees, tents, people, food, drink, stages, sights and smells lay ahead of them – yet incredibly, within ten minutes of walking, Kate had managed to bump into someone from work.

'Un-bloody-believable,' Emily announced. 'Only you.'

On the group walked, for miles and miles it seemed, swapping festival stories as they went – which meant Kate and Rachel just had to listen. The feeling of carefree festival happiness was soon washing over them like a warm waterfall. When they reached the Hare Krishna marquee Emily let out a little squeal.

'Ooh, you'll love it here!' she advised. 'Let's go in and chant along.'

Half an hour later, Kate had to be forcibly removed from the marquee by the others, as she was enjoying it so much. The simple feeling of something so totally different and almost out-of-body was somewhat addictive to Kate. She would have been happy in that marquee for the next four days!

By late afternoon they were all several drinks in and the dubious question of the infamous Glastonbury toilets came up. Kate was worried.

'They'll be fine today,' said Emily, assuring her sister that it probably wouldn't be until Saturday that things would get fairly grim. 'You have choices.' She went on to list the various toilet options.

First there was the Portaloo: less smelly in the mornings and a compact, bijou, private and fairly clean option. There was the rather off-putting story of a person found dead in one at the end of Glastonbury one year – and there was always the fear of being towed away while inside, no matter how unlikely that might be.

Then there was the long-drop: rows of green metal cubicles, inside which were wooden benches, each with a hole in. Beneath the hole, a drop of a few feet into a river of mixed human waste. A revolting concept, indeed a revolting sight if you dared look anywhere other than dead ahead – and unfortunately the most popular choice at Glastonbury, it seemed.

Next Emily described the compost toilet option. 'Like a cat litter tray: do your business, then cover it with bark.'

Urinals were apparently a possibility, too. Emily explained that these traditional troughs of urine were made accessible for women by use of a plastic pipe-like device, essentially giving the woman a 'penis' to pee from!

Finally, flushing toilets – these, Kate assumed, would be the obvious choice. However, Emily warned that they were housed in small caravan-like enclosures which harboured germs and smelled like nothing else. Worse, they tended to overflow, resulting in the need to wade through rivers of urine to get to one.

The rest of that first day was gloriously sunny. By early evening they were sitting on a hill overlooking the site, drinking the contents of their rucksacks, chatting and watching the world go by.

'Silent disco tonight,' announced Emily. 'You'll love it!'

Kate and Rachel had no concept of what a silent disco was at this stage, but they decided that wigs would be the thing they needed the most for such an event, so they went off on a small shopping trip. Trying on every wig they could find, they finally settled on a pair of matching ones, huge and curly: one electric blue and one purple. Kate had always had a penchant for a wig; somehow, wearing one gave her permission to be someone or anyone else. Significant events in her past had often been marked with the wearing of a wig: her hen night, her fortieth birthday, Nick's fortieth birthday, various fancy-dress parties. These had all provided the perfect opportunity to 'be someone else'. Tonight would be no different in this respect – she already felt like a different person anyway, due to the magic of Glastonbury.

'So you wear headphones and dance to whichever channel you tune to?' was Kate's incredulous response to Emily's instructions, as they stood in the queue for the silent disco later that night. By now it was approaching midnight and the group had arrived at the hugest marquee Kate had ever seen. 'But in reality, the dancefloor is silent?'

Kate was struggling with the concept, but she knew that if Emily rated this experience, it must be good. So, dressed in electric blue wig, palm tree T-shirt, blue denim shorts and walking boots, Kate took her neon flashing headphones, tuned into channel one and headed to the dancefloor. Once she got the hang of how to change the channel on her headphones, there was no stopping her: she was channel-surfing, dancing, singing and laughing the night away. There was a non-stop throng of moving bodies in the marquee throughout the night, the battle of the four DJs – one in each corner – raged continuously, and when one of them chose what was commonly accepted as an 'anthem' the crowd would simultaneously tune to the same channel and raise their fists to the air.

Hundreds of people came and went throughout the night. Eventually Emily and her posse left at around three o'clock. But Kate and Rachel were enjoying themselves so much that they stayed on. They lost count of the number of people who commented on their wigs, several actually thinking it was their real hair – which was more of a comment on their state of mind by that time of night than whether the wigs actually looked authentic. State of mind was an interesting concept for a slightly naive Kate at that point. She had never seen so many people openly taking drugs, in the most creative ways. It seemed that the utensil of choice for snorting cocaine was the innocent cotton-bud, while people inhaling laughing-gas from balloons was a totally new sight to her. Emily had had to explain to her earlier in the evening why so many people were 'blowing up' balloons.

The pair finally left the silent disco at about four-thirty and started the long walk back to their motor-home. Still on a natural high from the excitement of this new experience, they were chatting animatedly when a shadowy figure stepped out from behind one of the tents.

'All right, girls,' he said. 'Want some Ketamine?'

All Kate could do was laugh out loud, while Rachel thanked-but-no-thanked him and they walked on.

'What on earth would we do with a horse tranquiliser?' joked Kate.

The sun started to rise above the fields of Somerset. A warm glow surrounded them and they both agreed that this would be a moment they would remember for ever – without the help of mind-altering drugs!

Letter to Nick.

Well, that's the first time I've ever been offered Ketamine in my 43 years! I suppose we looked like fair candidates for it, walking along at 4.30 a.m. dressed in huge lairy wigs and gaping at the sunrise. I will probably dine out on that story for a lifetime.

Widow, 43
seeks her bed, as it's
been over twenty hours
since she last slept.

Chapter 21

Determined not to be counted as a lightweight on this trip, Kate dragged open her eyes after too few hours of sleep that morning, so that she could make an effort to join the group as planned around noon. This was the first day of wall-to-wall music spread across the twenty-odd stages and Emily had a heavy schedule lined up for them. Peering out of the motor-home window from her bed, she marvelled at the constant stream of people arriving. People of all different shapes and sizes, young and old. Family groups, friendship groups, hen parties, stag parties, couples, children skipping hand-in-hand and even toddlers being pulled along in what looked like small shopping trollies.

What her sleep had lacked in quantity, it had made up for in quality. Kate felt invigorated by one of the first nights she had slept through in the last twelve months that had left her feeling refreshed, rather than merely having her fatigue slightly abated.

There was much discussion about what footwear to adopt that day, as the sky looked a little threatening in the distance while they prepared for the long hike ahead. Shortly into their walk they encountered some seemingly dead bodies lying by the side of the path, which disconcerted the two festival-virgins. Emily and her friends walked on by as if it were perfectly normal and Kate was much relieved when one of them rolled over and groaned as she walked by.

'That could have been us,' Rachel remarked, remembering the Ketamine encounter only a few hours previously. The whole 900-acre site was slowly awakening and everyone was looking forward to a day of stage-hopping to find their favourite music and entertainment.

Unfortunately, Kate fell at the first hurdle. Having walked the several miles to the imaginatively-named Other Stage to watch the first act of their choice, she felt an immense wave of fatigue wash over her just as they arrived, so much so, that it nearly knocked her clean out. Was it the late night? Was it the last of the adrenaline that seemed to have been pumping through her body for weeks on end? Or was it simply that her body had tasted the sweetness that was pure, unadulterated sleep and wanted more? Whatever it was, Kate knew she had to get back to that motor-home and give in to this no matter what, so she made her excuses and left the group hastily. This was another example of what Kate regarded as her liberating outlook on life: she didn't care what people thought or said about her actions. She knew what she needed, and she went on and did it. It was also, she thought, another example of what you could do after being unexpectedly and unfairly widowed so young: people didn't judge or talk about your actions in the first place, anyway!

Hours and hours later Kate became vaguely aware of chattering and footsteps around her. It seemed she had slept all day and it was well into the evening already. The others had seemingly had a fun afternoon and were back for a quick wardrobe change and some food, and then planned to head back out to sample the after-dark delights of Glastonbury. Having shaken herself out of her slumber and now refreshed and ready for anything, Kate stepped out of the motor-home and straight into a huge puddle.

'What the hell?' she said, recoiling back into the motor-home. 'Where did this come from?'

She called over to Rachel, who was busy pulling on her long black rubber boots. For only in festival-world could one get away with a black crochet dress, wellingtons and a huge blue furry 'monster' hat. Kate had to admit that Rachel was rocking that look.

'Er... The huge electrical storm and about five hours of rain,' explained Rachel. 'I was so cold and wet by the time we walked back that I had to buy this to change into.' She was holding up the most hilarious tie-dye sweatshirt Kate had ever seen. They both looked at each other and collapsed in fits of laughter. Kate could simply not imagine Rachel wearing that item of clothing, for she was one of the most glamorous people Kate knew. But then they had both decided to embrace Glastonbury and go full hippie mode throughout, throwing caution to the wind (when it came to clothing, anyway). After further discussion it seemed that Kate had managed to sleep through the most terrible summer storm and thereby avoid the only rainfall that happened at that year's festival – an achievement which amused her no end.

The walk that night took the group via an area known as Arcadia. The thump, thump, thump of the music heralded their approach, and the nearer they got the further they waded into a sea of tiny silver canisters.

'Nitrous oxide,' Emily said, answering Kate's quizzical look. It seemed drug-taking had moved on several generations since Kate had last been 'on the scene' and the people she had seen the previous night sucking on balloons sourced their precious high from these tiny silver canisters which crushed and crunched under their feet as they walked.

'Oh right, yeah,' she shouted back over the music, trying to sound cool.

Suddenly three huge columns of flame leapt into the sky ahead of them, and the sight of an enormous metal spider which had housed the flames stopped them in their tracks. Standing, by Kate's reckoning, some seventy feet tall, the spider was a marvel of modern metal sculpture, with two huge red laser eyes which roved around the thousands of ravers who were gathering in the area.

These days Kate would never say the word 'ravers' aloud, knowing that this was an aged term relating to those heady Acid House days of the late 1980s and early 1990s. Before the era of widespread mobile phone usage, somehow 'word' would circulate that people were gathering in a certain field on a certain day. Thousands of people would turn up, mainly high on ecstasy, and rave the next twenty-four hours of their lives away. Dressed in day-glo tracksuits or large quantities of denim, paired with trainers and a whistle strung around the neck, these hedonistic thrill-seekers were the products of the 'greed is good' mantra from *Wall Street*. They were eating up life in huge quantities, draining it of everything for their own gratification, and they didn't care.

Arcadia certainly reminded her of the sights from those times: people dancing in a trance-like state to repetitive bass-line music, holding their hands aloft into a laser-light extravaganza, all set off by clouds of dry ice. The spider spat out fireworks and writhed its metal body above them, sending the crowd into a further frenzy of energetic dancing. It was an infectious atmosphere and Kate and the others joined in, absorbing the energy from around them and throwing their hands in the air, as if to worship the god of Glastonbury. Kate realised quickly that the reason ecstasy must have been so popular in the 1980s was that, in her opinion, no one could possibly sustain this level of activity without chemical enhancement. She soon bailed out, followed by the others shortly afterwards.

The rest of that night was a flurry of activity between different acts on different stages – so much to choose from, with huge distances to cover between stages. By now, they had walked and danced more miles than the infamous Three Peaks Challenge, and still with two more days to go, which Kate couldn't believe. She and Rachel had decided to play it safe that night and walk back shortly after Rudimental finished their set. The two of them knew they had an extremely full day of music planned for Saturday and did not want to miss a thing.

Back at the motor-home, Kate was feeling on top of the world. She bounded through the door and jumped onto her bed, which was the converted seating area of the vehicle. Crack, crack, bang went the wooden slats beneath her, leaving Kate sitting *in* the bed rather than on it!

After a fairly uncomfortable night's sleep, during which Kate found herself having to teeter on the edge of the bed to avoid falling in, the big day of music was upon them. Despite having so many stages to choose from, Kate and Rachel had agreed that they actually wanted to spend the whole day and night at the famous Pyramid Stage, where all the headline acts would play that day. It was hot and sunny, which made the subject of footwear tricky, as the huge downpour from the day before, mixed with hundreds of thousands of people on the land, had resulted in patches of slushy mud in the most popular areas. Not least by the toilets outside the Pyramid Stage, which seemed to have a river of urine gushing from them when Kate arrived, leaving her feeling distinctly nauseous. Seeking more acceptable toilets later that day, Kate found that Saturday was indeed the tipping point for all the toilets at Glastonbury, just as Emily had predicted, resulting in her having to stick pieces of tissue up her nose when using the facilities – much to the amusement of everyone else around her.

Choosing to spend the whole day at one stage worked well for Kate and Rachel. They found themselves able to move forward with each change of band, resulting in them being only four or five 'rows' back from the stage by the time Pharrell Williams came on. This was prime position, as the set was a real party piece. Uplifting wall-to-wall blockbuster hits energised the crowd and they danced and sang the late afternoon away. On the way to the Pyramid Stage the two of them had decided to purchase headwear to protect them from the heat of the day. They cut a real dash – or so they told themselves – that afternoon, resplendent in huge floppy straw hats, elaborately decorated in gaudy cloth flowers.

By the end of the Pharrell set, Kate had resolved to tough it out and wait for the headline act of the day, even though by that time they had been standing at the Pyramid Stage for several hours.

'We're at the front!' she squealed as the Pharrell fans started to leave. 'I can be that person on the telly,' she continued, 'having the time of my life at Glastonbury!'

Their position at the front was challenged several times during the following hour or so, as more and more Kanye West fans piled in. There was a notable change in the audience; they seemed rowdier and frequently the mass of the crowd would surge violently one way or the other, almost sweeping Kate right off her feet. Knowing that the Pyramid Stage could easily draw crowds of over 100,000 people, Kate didn't dare to look behind her as she jostled to retain her position and tried not to be crushed under people's feet.

'If this crowd surges like that one more time, I'm out,' she announced to Rachel, eyeing up the row of security guards who stood behind the metal barrier in front of them. Right on cue, the crowd started to surge forwards and sideways all at the same time, and right on cue, Kate shouted to the security guards: 'Get me out of here!' This was followed by the embarrassing spectacle of being hauled out of the crowd.

'Hold on to my neck!' shouted one of the security guards, as he grabbed Kate by her shorts and dragged her over the metal barrier, resulting in the most massive wedgie she had ever experienced.

'I'm sorry,' she apologised to Rachel as they both arrived, breathless, outside the crowd area. 'I wimped out.'

Kate wasn't sure whether Rachel was just being charitable that night, when she assured her that it was fine and she had wanted a drink and a pee anyway. Nonetheless, Kate felt they both breathed a sigh of relief as they walked away and went in search of food and drink.

Suitably revived towards the end of their marathon day, Kate had a flash of inspiration.

'Why don't we walk up to the Stone Circle for some chill-out time?' she suggested naively.

It was agreed and they set off, Kanye's dulcet tones ringing out behind them. As they walked towards the hill above the main site where the Stone Circle was situated, Kate was full of expectation. She felt that surely she would find some kind of inner peace in this magical-sounding place, and possibly even meet the Dalai Lama, who was rumoured to be attending that weekend. On reaching the top of the hill they found rocks, sure enough – but not the tranquil and serene atmosphere they were expecting. There were lots of shadowy figures lurking about amid an uneasy atmosphere. Suddenly a police van screamed into sight and about a dozen police officers ran past, collaring several people and dragging them towards the van.

'Let's go!' said Kate. They turned on their heels and walked briskly back down the hill.

Sunday was officially Lionel Richie day. There were plenty of other bands playing, of course, but Kate and her sister were most excited about seeing the former front man of the Commodores, even though that band had been a little before their time. As a homage to Lionel and his special brand of feel-good music, they all decided to don black wigs and moustaches, provided by Emily, who always had an eye for detail in these matters. Kate felt her wig was more Slash from Guns N' Roses than Lionel Richie, so she shoved some scissors into Rachel's hand and asked for a quick trim. Rachel was no hairdresser and it was the morning after (several) nights before, but what could possibly go wrong? Kate heard the snip, snip, snip as Rachel wielded the scissors with surprising dexterity, trying to fashion the long black curly wig into something more Lionel-like.

'Oh!' Rachel's voice came from behind Kate as she sat in the fold-up chair under the stripy green awning of the motor-home. Emily looked over and immediately grimaced, causing her black moustache to fall off, as the glue hadn't yet set.

'What?' asked Kate, totally oblivious to the unfolding situation as she basked in the morning sun. Emily's face said it all. Kate realised her mistake in not only wearing the wig while it was coiffured but also leaving her real hair loose underneath the wig while Rachel was armed with the scissors. Rachel held aloft a long piece of blonde hair and looked genuinely distressed and panicky. Kate remembered Nick joking about her having 'lost the edge' in her forties and felt the temptation of a fearsome reaction to prove this wasn't the case. Yet she surprised herself and everybody else that morning, when she simply said: 'Don't panic – it'll grow back.'

Everyone around her shared furtive glances. Kate thought she saw her sister mouthing 'She's gonna blow!' to Rachel, who was slowly backing away.

'Seriously,' Kate carried on. 'It's no biggie.' And she really meant it. If the past twelve months had taught her anything, it was that there was always something bigger and badder to worry about. So off they went, wigs and moustaches in place, to enjoy their day and see Lionel, who did not disappoint.

The group had agreed to gather once again at the Pyramid Stage that night, to watch The Who perform the closing set of the festival. It amused Kate to think she was going to watch a bunch of geriatrics performing hits that were written before she was even born, but she knew they would be worth the watch. They all convened in plenty of time to ensure they were at least in the front quarter of the crowd, in order to soak up the atmosphere of the whole experience. The wait was finally over and the opening chord of their opening song, the iconic and unmistakable 'Pinball Wizard', drove everyone wild. They all leapt in the air. For no obvious reason the woman behind them grabbed Rachel and started shouting at her. Kate couldn't make out what she was saying, but Rachel gave her short shrift and sent her packing.

Later that night, they laughed hard to discover from Rachel that the woman's issue had been the fact that their jumping had caused her to spill her precious cocaine.

'Who steps into the middle of a 100,000-strong crowd and expects to balance a minute amount of dust on a cotton bud with no spillage?' asked Kate. 'Priceless!'

Over the course of a few days Kate had learned a lot about people in crowd situations at festivals. There had also been the incident later on that night when the guy behind them had decided to pee there and then in the middle of the crowd, much to Kate's disgust. So maybe Kate wasn't a full-on festival queen, but she had experienced some excellent times that weekend and would probably dine out on the stories for years to come. She concluded that this would be her one and only trip to Glastonbury – but it was enough to last her a lifetime.

Letter to Nick.

That was a close call! I nearly got nicked this weekend. Who knew that the hallowed Stone Circle was where everyone goes to buy and sell drugs... Well not me, anyway! What the bloody hell was the Dalai Lama doing hanging round in a drug den after all? And as for the inner peace, I suppose we found it after we got our breath back at the bottom of the hill, having literally run away from the van full of police! We laughed and laughed, Nick. You'd have been proud, I think.

Widow, 43
seeks legal representation if
she continues at this rate!

Chapter 22

Thoroughly exhausted from the exertion of the Three Peaks Challenge, the excitement of Glastonbury and the despair at having reached that fateful anniversary of Nick's death, Kate mentally and physically collapsed for the rest of the summer months. It was a good time for a collapse, if ever there was one, as she could pass it off as sunbathing. Work had settled back into some kind of normality, after the upheaval of most of her team leaving while she had been off for the three months of the previous year, and as she headed into autumn Kate was beginning to feel that she had successfully re-established what 'normal' was for her now. 'Normal' was actually quite tranquil most of the time. The shocking events of fifteen months ago had left her with a new equanimity regarding most situations and had afforded her a new outlook on what she could cope with, which felt quite liberating. Nick had absolutely never impeded her progress or ambition in anything – in fact, quite the opposite – but Kate realised that he had always been a safety net, a fact which, by its very virtue, had slightly restricted how truly independent she had been.

Liberated, independent, exhilarated by the adventures she had taken during the summer months, and refreshed from her long 'sunbathe' afterwards, Kate therefore felt it was time to move on with her beloved house renovations. Having taken a long breather after all the work she had commissioned on the house the previous year, Kate decided the time was right to start the second phase – the final push to get it finished. She couldn't muster the enthusiasm to do any of it herself anymore, which saddened her a little; she and

Nick had worked their way through the previous two houses they had lived in, transforming them from dated and unloved buildings to their own little homes, becoming places that held so many good times over the years. The current project was going to be big by anyone's standards, but little did they know that within less than three years their project would be called to an abrupt halt. The irony of their last move, to this house of their dreams, had been Nick's declaration: 'That's it, I am *never* moving again. They'll have to carry me out in a box!' Kate had thought over the phrase 'Be careful what you wish for' a million times ever since. Kate had been the 'unskilled labour' of the partnership, whereas Nick had been the 'jack of all trades/turn his hand to anything' guy. So realistically, even if her heart was in it, her skill level definitely wasn't. She chuckled while writing the list of things she needed to include for the builders' quote, thinking of the time one sunny afternoon when she had helped Nick with some repair work on Harvey's stable opposite their back door. Her job had consisted exclusively of removing nails from pieces of wood – all bloody afternoon!

A friend had once described Kate's house as 'the money pit'. As she made her list, titled 'Everything that needs doing to finish this place', she realised he had been entirely correct. *House (inside)*; *House (outside)*: headings and sub-headings racked up like a bad gambler's debts. *Garden, stables, garages, barns, fencing, land, roofing, gates, driveway*. Underneath each sub-heading lay dozens of bullet points. Simply compiling the list was a major task in itself. *Trades needed: general builder, carpenter, plumber, electrician, landscaper, fencer, roofer, carpet-layer, decorator, tree surgeon, farmer…* and so it went on. After the list was finally complete, appointments for quotes had been booked and decisions had been taken, Kate felt she could take a holiday that autumn, safe in the knowledge that there would be a flurry of activity when she returned.

Their lucky Gran Canaria find the previous year had struck them all so positively that Kate, her sister and their mother had eagerly booked the same destination this year. Their return was a resounding success. Kate wondered if she would ever holiday with anyone but her mother and/or Emily ever again, but for now this was a happy and secure place to be, so she put these thoughts to the back of her head. The dynamic was, as usual, amusing: watching her mother and sister squabble on a daily basis about the most mundane things. Who ate the biscuit that came with Mum's hot chocolate each night? (Emily, when Mum wasn't looking.) Who left the wet towel on Em's sun-lounger? (Mum, when Emily wasn't looking.) However, the resort was just as tranquil as they remembered and the hotel, the sister to the one they had stayed at last year, was equally sumptuous, so there was simply nothing they didn't like about the whole experience – except the night flight back to England and the cold October weather that greeted them on their return.

Following a few short hours of sleep the day after their holiday, Kate dragged herself out of bed and decided some hot soup would warm her up nicely. Still in her pyjamas, with hair standing on end, she tucked into the most delicious bowl of curried vegetable soup and thought wistfully of the beautiful sunshine she had left behind less than twenty-four hours ago. Her ears pricked up as she heard a vehicle drive into the yard by the side of the house. Slightly grumpy at being simultaneously tired and having her lunch interrupted, Kate shuffled to the door and opened it, bowl of soup in hand. A tall man with a bowl-like haircut was getting out of a white pickup truck, smiling as if he knew her.

'Hi!' he announced. 'I'm Peter, from Fairoak Fencing.' When Kate looked blankly back, still shovelling soup into her mouth, he went on, slightly less assured this time. 'You asked me to measure up for fencing and gates?'

He was, of course, absolutely right. During her pre-holiday organisational flurry, Kate had popped into Fairoak Fencing on the way back from work one afternoon and asked them about repairing some of the fencing around the fields and gateways. Still unwilling to give up her soup, Kate slipped on some flipflops – impractical for walking around muddy fields and making an interesting complement to her tartan pyjamas – and stepped out to greet Peter.

As Kate and Fencing Man, as she had decided to think of him, walked around the areas that needed most urgent repair, they chatted. Or rather, he did the chatting while she finished her soup and pointed out everything she wanted doing. She paid little attention to the subject matter of his chatting, simply interjecting the odd 'Yes' or 'Oh really?' when it felt vaguely appropriate.

Peter's voice broke through Kate's indifferent wandering mind. 'Yes, I saw you in your fancy dress the other week.'

'Sorry?' came her reply. Her mind raced to think of parties she might have attended in the last few weeks and forgotten about. No, there definitely hadn't been any: Kate absolutely loved a fancy-dress party, so there was no way she would have forgotten one. Slightly indignantly, she continued, 'I definitely haven't been to any fancy-dress parties recently.'

'No, no,' reassured Fencing Man. 'You came in to book this appointment the other week, all done up in a fancy dress.'

Kate had completely got hold of the wrong end of the stick – he was talking about *a* fancy dress, not just *fancy dress*! A slight tinge of embarrassment crept up her cheeks as she started to explain about how she had come straight from work that day. Then, it suddenly dawned on her that she might actually be experiencing being chatted up for the first time in a long time. Her face must have registered her total shock – not only at being chatted up, but at actually not minding. Fencing Man must have mistaken her expression for offence, as he made his excuses and said something about 'just a bit of Friday afternoon fun', before jumping in his truck and driving off.

'So, this is it,' Kate thought as she walked back into the house. 'The turning-point.' This was the point at which she could consider the vague possibility of being chatted up and not instantly throw up. She thought back to the countless times over the past sixteen months when she had looked at couples and yearned for that companionship again, so deeply that it had made her breathless – yet when she had thought of spending time in the company of another man, the nausea had washed over her like a tidal wave. She also recalled that infamous conversation between Nick's father and brother, on the way the funeral, during which they had declared that she should move on and get married again. She had dismissed it at the time as ridiculous. 'But perhaps,' thought Kate now, 'it wasn't so ridiculous after all.'

Letter to Nick.

So, 486 days after you died I have been chatted up! Maybe I finally dropped the 'fuck off and die' look I seemed to have perfected for all men since I lost you. I actually think the nice man on the train chatted me up the other day too, but I was too busy arguing with him about whether I wanted sugar for my tea or not and didn't realise the implication was that I didn't need it because I was 'sweet enough' (until my travelling companion pointed it out). Perhaps there is life ahead of me.

Widow, 43
seeks a better 'chat-up
radar' if she's going
get on with life!

Chapter 23

Kate was in an awkward place. Aware now that she *could*, and possibly *should*, get on with her life, she was totally flummoxed as to *how*. She had weathered the immediate storm after Nick's death by battening down the hatches and, at first, merely existing. This had slowly progressed to living in the moment, and for many months that had been quite sufficient for her needs and wants. More recently, living in the moment had evolved into looking a little further ahead.

Since her revelation that she might actually quite enjoy 'stepping out' again, she wondered how on earth she would go about orchestrating it. 'First things first,' she said to herself as she looked in the mirror. 'You've got to smarten up.' Suddenly she realised Fit Plumber was due any minute, to do yet more work on the house's ancient pipes, during 'the final push' – as Kate had named the last of the building work. 'Bloody hell… I can't have him seeing me looking like this.'

Kate knew it wasn't a date. But she felt that if she really was going to move on in her life, she really needed to start giving a shit about what she looked like to the outside world – all the time, not just for evenings out, birthdays and gala dinners. Besides, this was Fit Plumber, so she thought he deserved a slight effort at least. Kate ran upstairs to change into some less war-torn jeans and possibly run the shower over her hair. Then she heard a van pull into the yard. 'Shit, he's here,' she thought, as she performed her quick-change. She was very adept at the quick-change, as she never, ever had enough time to cram everything she needed to do into one day. So she would often require three or four changes of clothes per day, which would usually go: horses (change 1), work (change 2), walk (change 3), horses again (change 4). Grabbing the dry shampoo, she thought she would come across as a little less unkempt if her hair didn't look so greasy. She sprayed it liberally with her right hand, while applying a generous spritz of perfume with her left. This went rather wrong, as such things so often did for Kate, and she managed to spray perfume in her eyes and totally overdo the dry shampoo, making her blonde locks look fairly grey all over. 'Bloody great...' she thought as she looked in the mirror at the bottom of the stairs. 'Now it looks like I have let myself go *and* I am going grey!'

The following weeks and then months passed by uneventfully. Work was interspersed with managing the house renovations; living in a building site became the everyday norm. In her quest to carry on changing her life and moving forward, Kate joined a gym. This was something she felt was a bit of a cliché, but having found that pilates offered great physical and mental benefits, she decided she needed to up things a gear or two and finally took the plunge, joining a swanky gym only fifteen minutes from her house. Things started very well: she found a fabulous class that she loved on Tuesday and Thursday evenings, which fused pilates with yoga and tai chi, led by the most positive and motivational teacher she had ever encountered. She was the type of woman Kate wanted to be but never would be. Lean and muscular, with a full-on six-pack, the teacher would spend the whole hour tying herself in impossible knots and balancing on one toe while singing along to the music – while Kate would be huffing and puffing, simply from getting into and out of the various poses she was attempting. Nevertheless, she loved the classes and found herself enjoying the fact that she wasn't just experiencing home–work–home five days a week.

A few weeks after joining, Kate was delayed at work and missed the precious start time for her Tuesday class. Disappointed, but determined not to be deterred from her new-found love of fitness, she decided to pop in to the gym on the way home anyway, to have a swim. It was getting quite late by then, but the upside to this was the fact that things tended to be a lot quieter and there was less chance of splashy kids in the pool. As she changed into her swimming costume she noticed that the lycra was starting to give out and made a mental note that she really must buy a new one. Scampering onto the poolside, to avoid being noticed by anyone in her shabby costume, she entered the pool on the lane-swimming side. This was unusual for Kate, as she would not normally prefer the discipline of keeping up with lane-swimmers, but it was the nearest side to the pool entrance. She felt she had to dive out of sight and get into the water quickly. 'Ok, Kate – you can do this,' she said to herself as she eyed up the determined-looking serious swimmers in her lane. It was at least the slow lane, and there were only two other people there, so she felt relatively confident that she would not be in anyone's way with her average-speed breaststroke. Kate liked to set herself goals when swimming; given that it had been a long day at work, she decided that twenty minutes would be ample swimming time, especially if she was keeping the pace up in the swim-lane.

Off she set, pulling herself through the water and relishing the exercise after so many hours in the car: kick, breathe, kick, breathe, kick, breathe. It was a great opportunity to have a good think about the day that had passed, the rest of the week ahead, life goals, what was on telly later… Ten minutes into her swim Kate saw what she could only describe as a Baywatch Babe enter the pool area. Resplendent in a red swimming costume, high-cut at the hip and generally skimpy in material, the woman was obviously a regular swimmer, with long muscular legs that propelled her easily and swiftly into the lane next to Kate – the one labelled 'Fast swimmers only – clockwise'. Baywatch Babe started off at great speed. As she approached Kate on the other side of the striped dividing rope, she caused a mini-tsunami of water ahead of her, which hit Kate just as she breathed in, causing her to choke and splutter momentarily. As Kate looked up, she realised to her horror that Baywatch Babe had been one of the 'mean girls' from school. For some reason, twenty-eight years after Kate had left that school, she was filled with dread.

'Did she recognise me?' was Kate's first thought. This soon turned to: 'Bloody typical – she had to look hotter than hot in a swimsuit, didn't she? Why is life so unfair?'

On Kate swam, while weighing up her options. 'I can't get out of the pool in front of Mean Girl Baywatch Babe. She'll see I've become fat… and old… and that I've got no bloody lycra left in my costume. Shit. I'll style it out and keep swimming until she gets out.' Later Kate would realise how irrational she had been: this woman probably wouldn't even know who Kate was – and anyway, what did it matter? But another twenty-five minutes passed and Kate found herself still swimming. By now it was a serious case of bloody-mindedness for Kate not to give in before Mean Girl Baywatch Babe. Shoulders aching and seriously out of puff by now, Kate kept soldiering on in her bid to remain anonymous. To her relief, Baywatch Babe stopped at one end of the pool and jumped lithely out onto the side. 'Phew,' Kate thought, while surreptitiously watching her walk along the edge of the pool. Just as Kate was planning her exit from this watery nightmare, Baywatch Babe stepped smilingly into the Jacuzzi at the far end of the swimming lane. Kate found herself channelling Grandad Leslie: 'Bloody bloody buggery bollocks!'

And so it came to pass that a whole hour after Kate had entered the pool for a nice little swim, she dragged herself out by the steps – no lithe jumping out of the water directly onto the poolside for her – and wobbled quite jelly-legged back to the changing room, for a good sit down and a reflection on what had just happened. Looking in the mirror at her red eyes and wrinkled skin, she pondered why her 'Who cares?' attitude had failed her so spectacularly and led to such a ridiculous situation. As she peeled off what remained of her greying and fraying black swimsuit and threw it in the bin, she concluded that her downfall stemmed from body confidence issues while unclothed. This brought her back to something she had been thinking about for a long time: that boob job she wanted. Right there and then Kate finally admitted it to herself. She wanted that reduction and she wanted it now.

Letter to Nick.

I spent a particularly long and boring telecon with the team at work today writing down the pros and cons of breast reduction. I felt it was time well spent, until Neil asked me a question and I had to fake a coughing-fit to get out of answering. Let's face it, this will not be a revelation to you. You watched me paint my nails during telecons... do my online shopping... and I even ran the hoover round the house during a particularly boring one. Work still gets in the way, Nick. Ironically, though, far less than it ever did before but too late for me to actually spend more precious moments with you. I remember that time you threatened to change your name to 'Paracetamol' in the hope that I would talk to you (or about you) more!

Widow, 43
seeks new swimsuit, new boobs and a new start.

Chapter 24

Four months and another birthday later Kate found herself in a hospital bed, waking up from surgery, feeling groggy with a strange mixture of hunger and nausea. The previous day had turned out to be an incredibly long one. Not permitted to eat from midnight the day before surgery, Kate had waited all day for her slot. As a consequence she was famished and incredibly faint by the time she had gone into theatre. That long wait had been spent reading her book, answering the many texts she had received, and simply pacing round the room in a bid to stave off thoughts about the risks of going under a general anaesthetic. The handsome anaesthetist had offered ample distraction from these thoughts earlier in the day, and provided the calm reassurance that people crave from medical professionals. But as the day had worn on, it had become harder for her to stay away from nagging doubts.

Kate's journey to this point had been quick and generally smooth. Once she had made the decision at the swimming pool that day, she had researched surgeons, booked appointments, stripped for way too many people along the way, and here she was only a few months later, job done and facing the start of a new phase in her life.

There had been a blip when she had announced her decision to Emily, whose reaction had been: 'Are you mad?' Kate had not seen that coming at all, but had discovered from it that her sister was certainly risk-averse when it came to matters of the physical. It had also been awkward telling her team at work why she was taking a couple of weeks out of the business. Believing in transparency and not wanting to worry anyone, she had told each of them the complete truth. Reactions ranged from 'Oh, that's awkward' to 'Well done you – you'll never look back.' Once again Kate had been surprised to find that everyone had an opinion or a story to share on the subject, just as she had experienced when she had embarked on the counselling two years earlier.

'How are you this morning?' a chirpy voice inquired, with an unmistakable Royal Tunbridge Wells accent. Looking at the clock on the wall opposite her bed, Kate noted that her surgeon was visiting at seven-thirty in the morning. She wondered whether he ever slept. He had greeted her on arrival at seven in the morning the previous day, had operated on her at six in the evening for the best part of two hours, and was back again this morning to check how she was. 'The beauty of private healthcare,' she thought. 'That and hot surgeons!'

'Oh, hi,' she replied, slowly dragging herself out of her slightly stupefied state.

As the surgeon started to examine his handiwork, all Kate registered him saying was that he had removed '1.5 kg in total'. Her head was swimming from the anaesthetic and she was still lurching from nausea to hunger, but her euphoria was clear and real when she looked down at her chest, which was, thankfully, half the size it had been. The physical relief was also considerable: no dragging feeling across her neck and shoulders any longer. She felt as though she had finally been allowed to put down the sack of coal she had been carrying for the past decade and she was so, so glad.

'Thank you so much,' she said, slightly tearfully. The surgeon must have been well-used to this type of reaction, as he merely smiled kindly and reiterated the instructions he had given previously about after-care.

Kate dozed off again shortly afterwards, before being woken up by a very efficient-sounding nurse bustling into the room.

'Right then, time to get up and about!' she announced. This didn't totally surprise Kate. She knew that the emphasis in all hospitals was around movement, thereby avoiding deep vein thrombosis.

However, she was surprised that the nurse didn't make any attempt to help her sit up or offer to assist her in any way. 'Come on then,' came the slightly impatient voice. 'You need to get into that shower.'

'Ok… Can you help me, please?' asked Kate, who generally didn't like to ask for help. But she really felt that after fairly major surgery and still feeling wobbly, it wasn't an unreasonable request. The nurse looked slightly aggrieved, which further surprised Kate as she slowly swung her legs round and out of the bed. She sat on the edge of the mattress and wondered what her next move would be.

The nurse enquired: 'Were you given any eye cream?'

Kate shook her head, partly to indicate 'No' in answer to the question, but also because she couldn't quite understand *why* she had been asked the question. Trying to rationalise the question in her mind, Kate wondered if anaesthetic caused dry eyes or something of the kind.

'Why would I need eye cream?' she went on to ask. There was a moment's silence in the room and an exchange of quizzical looks between the two women. Slowly a frown formed on Kate's face and her eyes narrowed. 'Do you think I have had *eye* surgery?' she asked, as a sinister realisation dawned on her. This private hospital in affluent Tunbridge Wells was packed full to the rafters with people – mainly women – trying to push back the hands of time, spending hard-earned cash on tummy tucks, breast surgery, liposuction, face-lifts… and, of course, plenty of eyelid-lifts. Kate tried to figure out if that was what the nurse thought she had had done. The answer was staring Kate in the face: the nurse turned a whiter shade of pale and excused herself immediately from the room. Swinging her legs as she sat in her pale blue hospital gown on the edge of the bed, Kate chuckled. 'Bloody hell… What would she have had me doing if I hadn't pointed out her error?' she asked herself. 'Bloody star-jumps?'

And so began a new adventure for Kate, starting much the same as any other for her: with a funny incident and a near-miss. Kate realised that the past two years had certainly been an interesting and varied journey – but they had provided her with the reassurance that she could cope with anything and everything that life deemed fit to throw at her.

Kate's only dilemma now was how to change the theory of moving on into the reality of moving on.

Letter to Nick.

I am ready for a new start. I still miss you immeasurably but in a different way now, less longing and with more memories that make me smile. I now no longer take solace in spinning your wedding ring round and round on my thumb, as if seeking the answer to some unasked question. I have taken my wedding ring off and yours and mine are living side-by-side in the blue flowered 'memory box'.

I am considering what life will bring me next, safe in the knowledge that I am in charge of my own destiny. I am also considering how my application to the Channel 4 show 'First Dates' will pan out. Em says that my first date in nineteen years shouldn't be in front of forty cameras and God knows how many viewers. Am I too old to get laid? I'm certain of one thing: I am too young to give up!

Widow, 44
seeks someone.

www.ingramcontent.com/pod-product-compliance
Lightning Source LLC
Chambersburg PA
CBHW030302100526
44590CB00012B/492